Daily Food for Christians

Daily Food

(Cover photograph by Mrs. Sharon White:
"View of the harbor at sunset, in Massachusetts.")

Daily Food

Daily Food for Christians

*Being a Promise and Another Scriptural Portion
for Every Day in the Year
Together with the Verse of a Hymn*

"I have esteemed the words of his mouth more than my necessary food." *Job 23:12.*

"Man doth not live by bread only, but by every word that proceedeth out of the mouth of the Lord doth man live." *Deut. 8:3, Matt 4:4.*

Daily Food

The text from the current edition was carefully transcribed from the 1800's edition, originally published by:
   THE AMERICAN TRACT SOCIETY, NY

Any additional images or text that has been added includes their source.

All Scripture Quotations are from the King James Bible.

Current edition, including photographs:
Copyright 2021 by Mrs. Sharon White and The Legacy of Home Press.

ISBN Number: 978-1-956616-06-4

The Legacy of Home Press

   Vermont - U.S.A.

Daily Food

Contents

Original "Daily Food" book   6

Preface   7

Daily Food

    January   9

    February   26

    March   42

    April   59

    May   75

    June   92

    July   108

    August   125

    September   142

    October   158

    November   175

    December   191

Appendix   211

Original Copy of "Daily Food"

Our copy of "Daily Food for Christians."

This edition has the original owner's signature, along with a date of 1868.

Preface

In the 1800's there was a miniature book published by the American Tract Society. It was very popular and was called, "Daily Food for Christians." It was a tiny book measuring only about 2 inches by 3 inches in size, but beautifully bound in hardcover. Some of these editions included the words, "I am the Bread of Life" on the cover, which referenced the Bible as being the nourishment we need for living.

The subtitle for this book described its contents: "Being a Promise and Another Scriptural Portion for Every Day in the Year Together with the Verse of a Hymn."

I first heard about this book when I was reading the 1882 edition of "The Life and Letters of Elizabeth Prentiss." Mrs. Prentiss owned one of these devotional books. It was given to her, as a gift, in 1835 when she was 17 years old. Many years later, she wrote about her love for the devotional in a letter to a friend in 1868:

"I have had this little book thirty-three years, it has travelled with me wherever I have been, and it has been indeed my song in the house of my pilgrimage."

Daily Food

Inside one of the blank pages of her copy of "Daily Food," she wrote the following lines:

> "Precious companion ! rendered dear
> By trial-hours of many a year,
> I love thee with a tenderness
> Which words have never yet defined."

We were able to obtain our own copy of one of these miniature books. It is fragile but well preserved. (A photograph can be seen on page 6.) I spent a great deal of time transcribing its contents into this larger, easier – to - read edition. I have also added beautiful illustrations of flowers, at the introduction of each month, from Currier & Ives. These drawings were published during the same time period in the 1800's.

May you be greatly blessed by the daily readings.

Mrs. Sharon White
The Legacy of Home Press, 2021

Daily Food

January

1 Roses and Bluebells

Daily Food

January

1. As thy days, so shall thy strength be.
Deut. 33:25.

To thy saints, while here below,
  With new years new mercies come;
But the happiest year they know
  Is the last which leads them home.

Be thou in the fear of the Lord all the day long.
Prov. 23:17.

January

2. My grace is sufficient for thee;
For my strength is made perfect in weakness.
2 Cor. 12:9.

I glory in infirmity,
  That Christ's own power may rest on me;
When I am weak, then I am strong;
  Grace is my shield; and Christ my song.

Hold thou me up, and I shall be safe.
  Psa. 119:117.

Daily Food

January

3. I am the Lord thy God, which teacheth thee to profit, which leadeth thee by the way that thou shouldest go.   *Isaiah 48:17.*

> Guide me, O thou great Jehovah,
>   Pilgrim through this barren land;
> I am weak, but thou art mighty,
>   Hold me by thy powerful hand.

Thou shalt guide me with thy counsel, and afterwards receive me to glory.   *Psalm 73:24.*

January

4. He that spared not his own Son, but delivered him up for us all, how shall he not with him also freely give us all things?   *Rom. 8:32.*

> My soul, ask what thou wilt,
>   Thou canst not be too bold;
> Since his own blood for thee he spilt,
>   What else can he withhold?

Lord, increase our faith.
Luke 17:5.

Daily Food

January

5. If thou canst believe, all things are possible to him that believeth. *Mark 9:23.*

O for a strong and lasting faith,
 To credit what the Almighty saith;
 To embrace the message of his Son,
 And call the joys of heaven my own.

Lord, I believe; help thou mine unbelief. *Mark 9:24.*

January

6. The Lord God is a sun and shield: the Lord will give grace and glory; no good thing will he withhold from them that walk uprightly. *Psalm 84:11.*

While fear hints, "There's something that God will deny,"
 "No good thing," is Faith's most decisive reply;
 Whate'er he withholds is most wisely denied;
 How full is the promise, "The Lord will provide!"

All things are yours.
 I Cor. 3:21.

January

7. In all thy ways acknowledge him, and he shall direct thy paths.   *Prov. 3:6.*

Each future scene to thee I leave;
  Sufficient 'tis to know
Thou canst from every evil save,
  And every good bestow.

Trust in the Lord will all thine heart; and lean not unto thine own understanding.   *Prov. 3:5.*

January

8. I give unto them [my sheep] eternal life; and they shall never perish, neither shall any pluck them out of my hand.   *John. 10:28.*

His honor is engaged to save
  The meanest of his sheep;
All that his heavenly Father gave,
  His hands securely keep.

My sheep hear my voice, and I know them, and they follow me.   *John 10:27.*

Daily Food

January

9. My God shall supply all your need according to his riches in glory by Christ Jesus. *Phil. 4:19.*

I can do all things, or can bear
  All sufferings, if my Lord be there;
Sweet pleasure mingles with the pains,
  While his right hand my head sustains.

I can do all things through Christ which strengtheneth me. *Phil. 4:13.*

January

10. All that the Father giveth me shall come to me; and him that cometh to me I will in no wise cast out. *John. 6:37.*

Come, ye sinners, poor and wretched,
  Weak and wounded, sick and sore;
Jesus ready stands to save you,
  Full of mercy joined with power: He is able,
He is willing, doubt no more.

Lord, to whom shall we go? thou hast the words of eternal life. *John 6:68.*

Daily Food

January

11. In the time of trouble he shall hide me in his pavilion; in the secret of his tabernacle shall he hide me; he shall set me up upon a rock.   *Psa. 27:5.*

The saints should never be dismayed,
 Nor sink in hopeless fear;
For when they least expect his aid,
 The Saviour will appear.

Thou hast been my help; leave me not, neither forsake me, O God of my salvation.   *Psalm 27:9.*

January

12. Wait on the Lord; be of good courage, and he shall strengthen thy heart.   *Psalm 27:14.*

O for a closer walk with God,
 A calm and heavenly frame;
A light to shine upon the road
 That leads me to the Lamb.

When thou saidst, Seek ye my face, my heart said unto thee, Thy face, Lord, will I seek.   *Psalm 27:8.*

Daily Food

January

13. He that shall endure unto the end, the same shall be saved.   *Matt. 24:13.*

Saints by the power of God are kept,
 Till his salvation come:
We walk by faith as strangers here,
 Till Christ shall call us home.

Watch therefore; for ye know not what hour your Lord doth come.   *Matt. 24:42.*

January

14. Whatsoever ye shall ask in my name, that will I do, that the Father may be glorified in the Son.   *John 14:13.*

Depend on Christ, thou canst not fail;
 Make all thy wants and wishes known:
Fear not; his merits shall prevail;
 Ask what thou wilt, it shall be done.

If ye love me, keep my commandments.   *John 14:15.*

Daily Food

January

15. There is therefore now no condemnation to them which are in Christ Jesus, who walk not after the flesh, but after the Spirit.   *Rom. 8:1.*

Who shall the Lord's elect condemn?
 'Tis God that justifies their souls,
And mercy, like a mighty stream,
 O'er all their sin divinely rolls.

If any man have not the Spirit of Christ, he is none of his.   *Rom. 8:9.*

January

16. There remaineth therefore a rest to the people of God.   *Heb. 4:9.*

Thine earthly Sabbaths, Lord, we love,
 But there's a nobler rest above;
To this our longing souls aspire
 With ardent pangs of strong desire.

Let us therefore fear, lest, a promise being left us of entering into his rest, any of you should seem to come short of it.   *Heb. 4:1.*

Daily Food

January

17. We have not a high-priest which cannot be touched with the feeling of our infirmities; but was in all points tempted like as we are, yet without sin. *Heb. 4:15.*

Touched with a sympathy within,
 He knows our feeble frame;
He knows what sore temptations mean,
 For he has felt the same.

Let us therefore come boldly unto the throne of grace, that we may obtain mercy, and find grace to help in time of need. *Heb. 4:16.*

January

18. They that know thy name will put their trust in thee. *Psalm 9:10.*

The men that know thy name will trust
 In thine abundant grace;
For thou hast ne'er forsook the just,
 That humbly seek thy face.

It is the Lord: let him do what seemeth him good. *I Sam. 3:18.*

Daily Food

January

19. If any man sin, we have an advocate with the Father, Jesus Christ the righteous; and he is the propitiation for our sins. *1 John 2:1, 2.*

He ever lives to intercede,
 Before his Father's face:
 Give him, my soul, thy cause to plead,
 Nor doubt the Father's grace.

Hereby we do know that we know him, if we keep his commandments. *1 John 2:3.*

January

20. Ask, and it shall be given you; seek, and ye shall find; knock, and it shall be opened unto you. *Luke 11:9.*

Encouraged by thy word
 Of promise to the poor,
Behold a beggar, Lord,
 Waits at thy mercy's door.
No hand, no heart, O Lord, but thine,
 Can help or pity wants like mine.

Lord, teach us to pray. *Luke 11:1.*

Daily Food

January

21. If ye then, being evil, know how to give good gifts unto your children, how much more shall your heavenly Father give the Holy Spirit to them that ask him?   *Luke 11:13.*

Come, Holy Spirit, heavenly dove,
  With all thy quickening powers;
Come, shed abroad a Saviour's love,
  And that shall kindle ours.

Grieve not the Holy Spirit of God.   *Eph. 4:30.*

January

22. Thou wilt keep him in perfect peace, whose mind is stayed on thee.   *Isaiah 26:3.*

From pole to pole let others roam,
  And search in vain for bliss;
My soul is satisfied at home,
  The Lord my portion is.

Trust ye in the Lord for ever; for in the Lord Jehovah is everlasting strength.   *Isaiah 26:4.*

Daily Food

January

23. I will heal their backsliding, I will love them freely; for mine anger is turned away.　*Hosea 14:4.*

How lost was my condition,
　Till Jesus made me whole;
There is but one Physician
　Can cure a sin-sick soul.

O Israel, return unto the Lord thy God; for thou hast fallen by thine iniquity.　*Hosea 14:1.*

January

24. Sin shall not have dominion over you; for ye are not under the law, but under grace.　*Rom. 6:14.*

When the load of sin is felt,
　And much forgiveness known;
Then the heart of course will melt,
　Though hard before as stone.

Let not sin therefore reign in your mortal body, that ye should obey it in the lusts thereof.　*Rom. 6:12.*

Daily Food

January

25. Being made free from sin, and become servants to God, ye have your fruit unto holiness, and the end everlasting life.   *Rom. 6:22.*

When from the curse God sets us free,
  He makes our nature clean;
Nor would he send his Son to be
  The minister of sin.

The wages of sin is death; but the gift of God is eternal life, through Jesus Christ our Lord.   *Rom. 6:23.*

January

26. Being confident of this very thing, that he which hath begun a good work in you, will perform it until the day of Jesus Christ.   *Phil. 1:6.*

Grace will complete what grace begins,
  To save from sorrows and from sins;
The work that Wisdom undertakes,
  Eternal Mercy ne'er forsakes.

Let your conversation be as it becometh the gospel of Christ.   *Phil. 1:27.*

January

27. God is faithful, who will not suffer you to be tempted above that ye are able; but will with the temptation also make a way to escape, that ye may be able to bear it.   *I Cor. 10:13.*

From trials none can be exempt,
  'Tis God's all-wise decree,
Satan the weakest saint will tempt,
  Nor is the strongest free.

Let him that thinketh he standeth, take heed lest he fall.   *I Cor. 10:12.*

January

28. When Christ, who is our life, shall appear, then shall ye also appear with him in glory.   *Col. 3:4.*

Lord, make us truly wise,
  To choose thy people's lot,
And earthly joys despise,
  Which soon will be forgot:
The greatest evil we can fear,
  Is to possess our portion here.

Set your affection on things above, not on things on the earth.   *Col. 3:2.*

Daily Food

January

29. Behold, the eye of the Lord is upon them that fear him, upon them that hope in his mercy. *Psa. 33:18.*

Amidst temptations sharp and long,
  My soul to this dear refuge flies;
Hope is my anchor, firm and strong,
  While tempests blow and billows rise.

Let thy mercy, O Lord, be upon us, according as we hope in thee. *Psa. 33:22.*

January

30. I will be a Father unto you, and ye shall be my sons and daughters, saith the Lord Almighty. *2 Cor. 6:18.*

Praise to the goodness of the Lord,
  Who rules his people by his word;
And there, as strong as his decrees,
  He sets his kindest promises.

Having therefore these promises, dearly beloved, let us cleanse ourselves from all filthiness of the flesh and spirit, perfecting holiness in the fear of God. *2 Cor. 7:1.*

Daily Food

January

31. Cast thy burden upon the Lord, and he shall sustain thee.   *Psalm 55:22.*

And shall I still the load retain,
 Which thou hast offered to sustain?
No; at thy bidding I will flee,
 And cast my burdens all on thee.

Casting all your care upon Him, for he careth for you. *I Peter 5:7.*

Daily Food

February

2 Moss, Roses, and Buds

Daily Food

February

1. The Lord is my strength and song, and he is become my salvation. *Exod. 15:2.*

To those who fear and trust the Lord,
 His mercy stands for ever sure;
From age to age his promise lives,
 And the performance is secure.

What time I am afraid, I will trust in thee. *Psalm 56:3.*

February

2. The Lord's portion is his people. Jacob is the lot of his inheritance. *Deut. 32:9.*

The Lord my portion is,
 I shall be well supplied;
Since he is mine, and I am his,
 What can I want beside?

Save thy people, and bless thine inheritance; feed them also, and lift them up for ever. *Psalm 28:9.*

Daily Food

February

3. The eternal God is thy refuge, and underneath are the everlasting arms.   *Deut. 33:27.*

God is the refuge of his saints,
  When storms of sharp distress invade;
Ere we can offer our complaints,
  Behold him present with his aid.

Now unto him that is able to keep you from falling, and to present you faultless before the presence of his glory with exceeding joy, to the only wise God our Saviour, be glory and majesty, dominion and power, both now and ever. Amen.   *Jude 24, 25.*

February

4. He will keep the feet of his saints.   *I Sam. 2:9.*

Order my footsteps by thy word,
  And make my heart sincere:
Let sin have no dominion, Lord,
  But keep my conscience clear.

Hold up my goings in thy paths, that my footsteps slip not.   *Psa. 17:5.*

February

5. If thou seek him, he will be found of thee; but if thou forsake him, he will cast thee off for ever.
I Chron. 28:9.

Soon as I heard my Father say,
 "Ye children, seek my grace,"
My heart replied without delay,
 "I'll seek my Father's face."

Know thou the God of thy father, and serve him with a perfect heart, and with a willing mind. *I Chr. 28:9.*

February

6. Acquaint now thyself with him, and be at peace; thereby good shall come unto thee. *Job 22:21.*

Blind unbelief is sure to err,
 And scan his work in vain;
God is his own interpreter,
 And he will make it plain.

That which I see not, teach thou me: if I have done iniquity, I will do no more. *Job 34:32.*

Daily Food

February

7. Thus saith the high and lofty One that inhabiteth eternity, whose name is Holy: I dwell in the high and holy place, with him also that is of a contrite and humble spirit, to revive the spirit of the humble, and to revive the heart of the contrite ones.   *Isa. 57:15.*

A broken heart, my God, my King,
  Is all the sacrifice I bring;
 The God of grace will ne'er despise
  A broken heart for sacrifice.

Be clothed with humility.   *I Pet. 5:5.*

February

8. God resisteth the proud, and giveth grace to the humble.   *I Pet. 5:5.*

As a little child relies
  On a care beyond his own;
 Knows he's neither strong nor wise,
  Fears to stir a step alone:
Let me thus with thee abide,
  As my Father, Guard, and Guide.

Humble yourselves therefore under the mighty hand of God, that he may exalt you in due time.   *I Pet. 5:6.*

Daily Food

February

9. I am the resurrection and the life: he that believeth in me, though he were dead, yet shall he live; and whosoever liveth, and believeth in me, shall never die.   *John 11:25, 26.*

My flesh shall slumber in the ground,
  Till the last trumpet's joyful sound;
 Then burst the chains with sweet surprise,
  And in my Saviour's image rise.

Though after my skin worms destroy this body, yet in my flesh shall I see God.   *Job 19:26.*

February

10. Surely I know that it shall be well with them that fear God.   *Eccl. 8:12.*

His mercy never shall remove
  From men of heart sincere;
 He saves the souls whose humble love
  Is joined with holy fear.

God be merciful to me a sinner.   *Luke 18:13*
.

Daily Food

February

11. In whom we have redemption through his blood, even the forgiveness of sins.   *Col. 1:14.*

Which of all our friends, to save us,
  Could or would have shed his blood?
 But our Jesus died to have us
  Reconciled in him to God:
This was boundless love indeed,
  Jesus is a friend in need.

Walk worthy of the Lord unto all pleasing, being fruitful in every good work, and increasing in the knowledge of God.   *Col. 1:10.*

February

12. They that trust in the Lord shall be as mount Zion, which cannot be removed, but abideth for ever. *Psalm 125:1.*

Mere mortal power shall fade and die,
  And youthful vigor cease;
 But we that wait upon the Lord
  Shall feel our strength increase.

He that trusteth in his own heart is a fool. *Prov. 28:26.*

February

13. He shall redeem Israel from all his iniquities.
Psalm 130:8.

Believing, we rejoice
 To see the curse remove;
We bless the Lamb with cheerful voice,
 And sing his bleeding love.

Christ hath redeemed us from the curse of the law, being made a curse for us.   *Gal. 3:13.*

February

14. In my Father's house are many mansions: if it were not so, I would have told you. I go to prepare a place for you.   *John 14:2.*

O glorious hour! O blest abode!
 I shall be near and like my God;
And flesh and sin no more control
 The sacred pleasures of the soul.

We know that if our earthly house of this tabernacle were dissolved, we have a building of God, a house not made with hands, eternal in the heavens.
2 Cor. 5:1.

Daily Food

February

15. Fear not, thou worm Jacob, and ye men of Israel; I will help thee, saith the Lord, and thy Redeemer, the Holy One of Israel.   *Isa. 41:14.*

Ye fearful saints, fresh courage take,
　The clouds ye so much dread
Are big with mercies, and shall break
　In blessings on your head.

I glory in my infirmities, that the power of Christ may rest upon me.   *2 Cor. 12:9.*

February

16. As the mountains are round about Jerusalem, so the Lord is round about his people from henceforth even for ever.   *Psalm 125:2.*

Firm as the earth thy gospel stands,
　My Lord, my hope, my trust;
If I am found in Jesus' hands,
　My soul can ne'er be lost.

Give us help from trouble, for vain is the help of man. *Psalm 60:11.*

February

17. Can a woman forget her sucking child, that she should not have compassion on the son of her womb? yea, they may forget, yet will I not forget thee.
Isaiah 49:15.

Can a mother's tender care
  Cease towards the child she bare?
Yes, she may forgetful be,
  Yet will I remember thee.

Cease ye from man, whose breath is in his nostrils; for wherein is he to be accounted of? *Isaiah 2:22.*

February

18. Thou art a God ready to pardon, gracious and merciful, slow to anger, and of great kindness.
Neh. 9:17.

Whate'er thy providence denies,
  I calmly would resign;
For thou art just and good and wise;
  O bend my will to thine.

Bless the Lord, O my soul. *Psalm 103:22.*

Daily Food

February

19. Who is among you that feareth the Lord, that obeyeth the voice of his servant, that walketh in darkness, and hath no light? let him trust in the name of the Lord, and stay upon his God.   *Isaiah 50:10.*

Judge not the Lord by feeble sense,
  But trust him for his grace;
Behind a frowning providence
  He hides a smiling face.

Though he slay me, yet will I trust in him.   *Job 13:15.*

February

20. Christ was once offered to bear the sins of many; and unto them that look for him shall he appear the second time without sin unto salvation.   *Heb. 9:28.*

It cost him death to save our lives,
  To buy our souls it cost his own;
And all the unknown joys he gives,
  Were bought with agonies unknown.

Be patient therefore, brethren, unto the coming of the Lord.   *Jas. 5:7.*

Daily Food

February

21. The Lord is very pitiful, and of tender mercy. *James 5:11.*

Trials must and will befall;
But, with humble faith, to see
Love inscribed upon them all -
This is happiness to me.

Take, my brethren, the prophets, who have spoken in the name of the Lord, for an example of suffering affliction, and of patience. *Jas. 5:10.*

February

22. I have blotted out, as a thick cloud, thy transgressions, and as a cloud, thy sins: return unto me, for I have redeemed thee. *Isa. 44:22.*

Blest is the man, for ever blest,
Whose guilt is pardoned by his God;
Whose sins with sorrow are confessed,
And covered with his Saviour's blood.

The blood of Jesus Christ his Son cleanseth us from all sin. *I John 1:7.*

February

23. I am persuaded, that neither death, nor life, nor angels, nor principalities, nor powers, nor things present, nor things to come, nor height, nor depth, nor any other creature, shall be able to separate us from the love of God which is in Christ Jesus our Lord. *Rom. 8:38, 39.*

Not all that men on earth can do,
  Nor powers on high, nor powers below,
Shall cause his mercy to remove,
  Or wean our hearts from Christ our love.

So shall we ever be with the Lord. *I Thess. 4:17.*

February

24. The effectual fervent prayer of a righteous man availeth much. *Jas. 5:16.*

Prayer an answer will obtain,
  Though the Lord a while delay;
None shall seek his name in vain,
  None be empty sent away.

Pray one for another. *James 5:16.*

February

25. He shall deliver thee in six troubles; yea, in seven there shall no evil touch thee.   *Job 5:19.*

In the furnace God may prove thee,
  Thence to bring thee forth more bright;
But can never cease to love thee,
  Thou art precious in his sight:
God is with thee,
  God thine everlasting light.

Happy is the man whom God correcteth; therefore despise not thou the chastening of the Almighty.
Job 5:17.

February

26. God hath not appointed us to wrath, but to obtain salvation by our Lord Jesus Christ.   *I Thess. 5:9.*

Be all my heart and all my days
  Devoted to my Saviour's praise;
And let my glad obedience prove
  How much I owe, how much I love.

Rejoice evermore.   *I Thess. 5:16.*

Daily Food

February

27. Like as a father pitieth his children, so the Lord pitieth them that fear him; for he knoweth our frame, he remembereth that we are dust.   *Psalm 103:13, 14.*

The pity of the Lord,
  To those that fear his name,
Is such as tender parents feel -
  He knows our feeble frame.

O Lord, thou art our Father; we are the clay, and thou our potter; and we all are the work of thy hand.
Isaiah 64:8.

February

28. If thou, Lord, shouldest mark iniquities, O Lord, who shall stand?   *Psalm 130:3.*

Great God, should thine all-seeing eye,
  And thine impartial hand,
Mark and revenge iniquity,
  No mortal flesh could stand.

But there is forgiveness with thee, that thou mayest be feared.   *Psalm 130:4.*

Daily Food

February

29. LEAP-YEAR. It is of the Lord's mercies that we are not consumed, because his compassions fail not. They are new every morning: great is thy faithfulness. *Lam. 3:22, 23.*

If, under means of grace,
  No fruits of grace appear,
It is a dreadful case:
  Though God may long forbear,
At length he'll strike the threatened blow,
  And lay the barren fig-tree low.

Then said he unto the dresser of his vineyard, Behold, these three years I come seeking fruit on this fig-tree, and find none: cut it down; why cumbereth it the ground? And he answering, said unto him, Lord, let it alone this year also, till I shall dig about it, and dung it: and if it bear fruit, well; and if not, then after that thou shalt cut it down.   *Luke 13:7-9.*

Daily Food

March

3 Feast of Roses.

Daily Food

March

1. My times are in thy hand.   *Psa. 31:15.*

My times are in thy hand,
  Whatever they may be,
Pleasing or painful, dark or bright,
  As best may seem to thee.

Make thy face to shine upon thy servant; save me, for thy mercies' sake.   *Psalm 31:16.*

March

2. The Lord will be a refuge for the oppressed, a refuge in times of trouble.   *Psalm 9:9.*

Other refuge have I none,
  Hangs my only hope on thee;
Leave, O leave me not alone,
  Still support and comfort me.

Thou, Lord, hast not forsaken them that seek thee.
Psalm 9:10.

Daily Food

March

3. The meek will he guide in judgment, and the meek will he teach his way. *Psalm 25:9.*

O that the Lord would guide my ways,
 To keep his statutes still;
O that my God would grant me grace
 To know and do his will.

Show me thy ways, O Lord; teach me thy paths. *Psalm 25:4.*

March

4. Blessed are the poor in spirit, for theirs is the kingdom of heaven. *Matt. 5:3.*

Blest are the humble souls that see
 Their emptiness and poverty:
Treasures of grace to them are given,
 And crowns of joy laid up in heaven.

Except a man be born again, he cannot see the kingdom of God. *John 3:3.*

Daily Food

March

5. Blessed are they that mourn; for they shall be comforted. *Matt. 5:4.*

Blest are the men of broken heart,
 Who mourn for sin with inward smart;
The blood of Christ divinely flows,
 A healing balm for all their woes.

Godly sorrow worketh repentance to salvation not to be repented of; but the sorrow of the world worketh death. *2 Cor. 7:10.*

March

6. Blessed are the meek; for they shall inherit the earth. *Matt. 5:5.*

Blest are the meek who stand afar
 From rage and passion, noise and war;
God will secure their happy state,
 And plead their cause against the great.

Verily, I say unto you, Except ye be converted, and become as little children, ye shall not enter into the kingdom of heaven. *Matt. 18:3.*

Daily Food

March

7. Blessed are they which do hunger and thirst after righteousness; for they shall be filled.   *Matt. 5:6.*

 Blest are the souls that thirst for grace,
  Hunger and long for righteousness;
 They shall be well supplied and fed
  With living streams and living bread.

How sweet are thy words unto my taste! yea, sweeter than honey to my mouth.   *Psalm 119:103.*

March

8. Blessed are the merciful; for they shall obtain mercy.   *Matt. 5:7.*

 Blest are the men whose feelings move,
  And melt with sympathy and love;
 From Christ the Lord shall they obtain
  Like sympathy and love again.

Be ye kind one to another, tender-hearted, forgiving one another, even as God for Christ's sake hath forgiven you.   *Eph. 4:32.*

March

9. Blessed are the pure in heart; for they shall see God.   *Matt. 5:8.*

Blest are the pure whose hearts are clean
 From the defiling power of sin;
With endless pleasure they shall see
 A God of spotless purity.

Who can understand his errors? cleanse thou me from secret faults.   *Psalm 19:12.*

March

10. Blessed are the peacemakers; for they shall be called the children of God.   *Matt. 5:9.*

Blest are the men of peaceful life,
 Who quench the coals of growing strife;
They shall be called the heirs of bliss,
 The sons of God, the sons of peace.

Follow peace with all men, and holiness, without which no man shall see the Lord.   *Heb. 12:14.*

Daily Food

March

11. Blessed are they which are persecuted for righteousness' sake; for theirs is the kingdom of heaven.   *Matt. 5:10.*

Blest are the sufferers who partake
 Of pain and shame for Jesus' sake;
 Their souls shall triumph in the Lord,
 Glory and joy are their reward.

Endure hardness, as a good soldier of Jesus Christ.
2 Tim. 2:3.

March

12. Light is sown for the righteous, and gladness for the upright in heart.   *Psalm 97:11.*

Immortal light and joys unknown,
 Are for the saints in darkness sown;
 Those glorious seeds shall spring and rise,
 And the bright harvest bless our eyes.

Rejoice in the Lord, ye righteous; and give thanks at the remembrance of his holiness.   *Psalm 97:12.*

Daily Food

March

13. The Lord is good, his mercy is everlasting, and his truth endureth to all generations. *Psalm 100:5.*

Wide as the world is thy command;
 Vast as eternity thy love;
Firm as a rock thy truth must stand,
 When rolling years shall cease to move.

Serve the Lord with gladness. *Psa. 100:2.*

March

14. He will regard the prayer of the destitute, and not despise their prayer. *Psalm 102:17.*

He frees the souls condemned to death,
 And when his saints complain,
It sha'n't be said, that "praying breath
 Was ever spent in vain."

Hide not thy face from me in the day when I am in trouble. *Psalm 102:2.*

Daily Food

March

15. The Lord is merciful and gracious, slow to anger, and plenteous in mercy. *Psalm 103:8.*

My soul, repeat His praise,
  Whose mercies are so great;
Whose anger is so slow to rise,
  So ready to abate.

Bless the Lord, O my soul; and all that is within me, bless his holy name. *Psalm 103:1.*

March

16. The mercy of the Lord is from everlasting to everlasting upon them that fear him. *Psalm 103:17.*

O God, our help in ages past,
  Our hope for years to come,
Be thou our guard while troubles last,
  And our eternal home.

The fear of the Lord is the beginning of wisdom.
Psalm 111:10.

Daily Food

March

17. Say ye to the righteous, that it shall be well with him.   *Isaiah 3:10.*

Rejoice, ye righteous, and record
 The sacred honors of the Lord;
 None but the soul that feels his grace,
 Can triumph in his holiness.

Woe unto the wicked; it shall be ill with him.
Isaiah 3:11.

March

18. Behold, God is my salvation; I will trust, and not be afraid: for the Lord Jehovah is my strength and my song; he also is become my salvation.
Isaiah 12:2.

Our God, how firm his promise stands,
 E'en when he hides his face;
 He trusts in our Redeemer's hands
 His glory and his grace.

O Lord, I will praise thee: though thou wast angry with me, thine anger is turned away, and thou comfortedst me.   *Isaiah 12:1.*

Daily Food

March

19. A bruised reed shall he not break, and smoking flax shall he not quench, till he send forth judgment unto victory. *Matt. 12:20.*

He'll never quench the smoking flax,
  But raise it to a flame;
The bruised reed he never breaks,
  Nor scorns the meanest name.

Himself took our infirmities, and bare our sicknesses. *Matt. 8:17.*

March

20. Come unto me, all ye that labor and are heavy-laden, and I will give you rest. *Matt. 11:28.*

Come hither, all ye weary souls.
  Ye heavy-laden sinners, come;
I'll give you rest from all your toils,
  And raise you to my heavenly home.

We which have believed do enter into rest. *Heb. 4:3.*

Daily Food

March

21. Whosoever shall confess me before men, him will I confess also before my Father which is in heaven. *Matt.10:32.*

Jesus, and shall it ever be,
 A mortal man ashamed of thee?
Ashamed of thee, whom angels praise,
 Whose glories shine through endless days?

Whosoever shall deny me before men, him will I also deny before my Father which is in heaven.
Matt. 10:33.

March

22. Where sin abounded, grace did much more abound. *Rom. 5:20.*

Where sin did reign, and death abound,
 There have the sons of Adam found
Abounding life; there glorious grace
 Reigns through the Lord our righteousness.

That as sin hath reigned unto death, even so might grace reign through righteousness unto eternal life, by Jesus Christ our Lord. *Rom. 5:21.*

Daily Food

March

23. As many as are led by the Spirit of God, they are the sons of God.   *Rom.8:14.*

Assure my conscience of her part
 In the Redeemer's blood,
 And bear thy witness with my heart,
  That I am born of God.

Ye have not received the spirit of bondage again to fear; but ye have received the Spirit of adoption, whereby we cry, Abba, Father.
Rom. 8:15.

March

24. The Spirit itself beareth witness with our spirit, that we are the children of God.   *Rom. 8:16.*

Dost thou not dwell in all the saints,
 And seal the heirs of heaven?
 When wilt thou banish my complaints,
 And show my sins forgiven?

If children, then heirs; heirs of God, and joint-heirs with Christ.   *Rom. 8:17.*

March

25. The sufferings of this present time are not worthy to be compared with the glory which shall be revealed in us.   *Rom.8:18.*

When overwhelmed with grief,
 My heart within me dies,
Helpless, and far from all relief,
 To heaven I lift mine eyes.

Rejoice in the Lord, O ye righteous; for praise is comely for the upright.   *Psalm 33:1.*

March

26. If we confess our sins, he is faithful and just to forgive us our sins, and to cleanse us from all unrighteousness.   *1 John 1:9.*

While I concealed my guilt,
 I felt the festering wound,
Till I confessed my sins to thee,
 And ready pardon found.

If we say that we have not sinned, we make him a liar, and his word is not in us.   *1 John 1:10.*

Daily Food

March

27. In this was manifested the love of God toward us, because that God sent his only-begotten Son into the world, that we might live through him.
I John 4:9.

Thy cruel thorns, thy shameful cross,
  Procure us heavenly crowns;
 Our highest gain springs from thy loss,
  Our healing from thy wounds.

Beloved, if God so loved us, we ought also to love one another. *I John 4:11.*

March

28. God is love; and he that dwelleth in love, dwelleth in God, and God in him. *I John 4:16.*

Were the whole realm of nature mine,
  That were a present far too small;
 Love so amazing, so divine,
  Demands my soul, my life, my all.

We love him, because he first loved us.
I John 4:19.

March

29. The Lord is my defence, and my God is the rock of my refuge. *Psalm 94:22.*

Poor though I am, despised, forgot,
 Yet God, my God, forgets me not;
And he is safe, and must succeed,
 For whom the Lord vouchsafes to plead.

When I said, My foot slippeth; thy mercy, O Lord, held me up. *Psalm 94:18.*

March

30. Him that overcometh, will I make a pillar in the temple of my God, and he shall go no more out. *Rev. 3:12.*

Then let my soul march boldly on,
 Press forward to the heavenly gate;
There peace and joy eternal reign,
 And glittering robes for conquerors wait.

Hold that fast which thou hast, that no man take thy crown. *Rev. 3:11.*

Daily Food

March

31. To him that overcometh will I give to eat of the tree of life, which is in the midst of the paradise of God. *Rev.2:7.*

Yes, while the dear Redeemer lives,
 We have a boundless store,
And shall be fed with what he gives,
 Who lives for evermore.

Unto him that loved us, and washed us from our sins in his own blood, and hath made us kings and priests unto God and his Father; to him be glory and dominion for ever and ever. Amen.
Rev. 1:5, 6.

Daily Food

April

4 Roses and Rosebuds

Daily Food

April

1. Justice and judgment are the habitation of thy throne; mercy and truth shall go before thy face.
Psa. 89:14.

Justice and judgment are thy throne,
  Yet wondrous is thy grace;
While truth and mercy, joined in one,
  Invite us near thy face.

Christ also hath once suffered for sins, the just for the unjust, that he might bring us to God.
I Peter 3:18.

April

2. He giveth power to the faint, and to them that have no might he increaseth strength. *Isaiah 40:29.*

When sore afflictions press me down,
  I need thy quickening powers:
Thy word, that I have rested on,
  Shall help my heaviest hours.

In God have I put my trust: I will not be afraid what man can do unto me. *Psalm 56:11.*

Daily Food

April

3. He shall feed his flock like a shepherd: he shall gather the lambs with his arm, and carry them in his bosom. *Isaiah 40:11.*

When faint and trembling with alarms,
 O gather us within thine arms;
Kind Shepherd, on thy gracious breast
 The weakest lamb may safely rest.

I am the good Shepherd: the good Shepherd giveth his life for the sheep. *John 10:11.*

April

4. Blessed is the people that know the joyful sound: they shall walk, O Lord, in the light of thy countenance. *Psalm 89:15.*

Blest are the souls that hear and know
 The gospel's joyful sound;
Peace shall attend the path they go,
 And light their steps surround.

In thy name shall they rejoice all the day, and in thy righteousness shall they be exalted. *Psalm 89:16.*

Daily Food

April

5. They that wait upon the Lord shall renew their strength; they shall mount up with wings as eagles; they shall run, and not be weary; and they shall walk, and not faint. *Isa. 40:31.*

Swift as an eagle cuts the air,
 We'll mount aloft to thine abode;
On wings of love our souls shall fly,
 Nor tire amidst the heavenly road.

My soul, wait thou only upon God; for my expectation is from him. *Psa. 62:5.*

April

6. The Lord's hand is not shortened, that it cannot save; neither his ear heavy, that it cannot hear.
Isa. 59:1.

Wait on the Lord, ye trembling saints,
 And keep your courage up;
He'll raise your spirit when it faints,
 And far exceed your hope.

Fight the good fight of faith, lay hold on eternal life.
I Tim 6:12.

Daily Food

April

7. When the enemy shall come in like a flood, the Spirit of the Lord shall lift up a standard against him. *Isa. 59:19.*

Restraining prayer, we cease to fight;
 Prayer makes the Christian's armor bright,
And Satan trembles when he sees
 The weakest saint upon his knees.

Resist the devil, and he will flee from you.
James 4:7.

April

8. Blessed is the man that trusteth in the Lord, and whose hope the Lord is. *Jer. 17:7.*

Begone, unbelief, my Saviour is near,
 And for my relief will surely appear;
By faith let me wrestle, and he will perform;
 With Christ in the vessel, I smile at the storm.

Cursed be the man that trusteth in man, and maketh flesh his arm, and whose heart departeth from the Lord. *Jer.17:5*

Daily Food

April

9. Heal me, O Lord, and I shall be healed; save me, and I shall be saved: for thou art my praise. *Jer. 17:14.*

A guilty, weak, and helpless worm,
  On thy kind arms I fall:
 Be thou my strength and righteousness,
  My Jesus, and my all.

O Lord, the hope of Israel, all that forsake thee shall be ashamed, and they that depart from me shall be written in the earth, because they have forsaken the Lord, the fountain of living waters. *Jer. 17:13.*

April

10. O Israel, thou hast destroyed thyself; but in me is thy help. *Hos. 13:9.*

Could the creatures help or ease us,
  Seldom should we think of prayer;
 Few, if any, come to Jesus,
  Till reduced to self-despair.

When we were yet without strength, in due time Christ died for the ungodly. *Rom. 5:6.*

April

11. The Lord is good unto them that wait for him, to the soul that seeketh him. *Lam. 3:25.*

Did ever mourner plead with thee,
 And thou refuse that mourner's plea?
Does not the word still fixed remain,
 That none shall seek thy face in vain?

It is good that a man should both hope and quietly wait for the salvation of the Lord. *Lam. 3:26.*

April

12. Because thou hast been my help, therefore in the shadow of thy wings will I rejoice. *Psalm 63:7.*

His love in time past forbids me to think
 He'll leave me at last in trouble to sink:
Each sweet Ebenezer I have in review,
 Confirms his good pleasure to help me quite through.

The Lord is my portion, saith my soul; therefore will I hope in him. *Lam. 3:24.*

Daily Food

April

13. Then shall we know, if we follow on to know the Lord. *Hos. 6:3.*

I need the influence of thy grace,
 To speed me in my way;
Lest I should loiter in my race,
 Or turn my feet astray.

No man having put his hand to the plough, and looking back, is fit for the kingdom of God.
Luke 9:62.

April

14. When I sit in darkness, the Lord shall be a light unto me. *Micah 7:8.*

Though dark be my way, since He is my guide,
 'Tis mine to obey, 'tis His to provide;
Though cisterns be broken, and creatures all fail,
 The word he has spoken shall surely prevail.

I will bear the indignation of the Lord, because I have sinned against him, until he plead my cause, and execute judgment for me. *Mic. 7:9*

April

15. I will look unto the Lord; I will wait for the God of my salvation; my God will hear me.
Micah 7:7.

When I am filled with sore distress
 For some surprising sin,
I'll plead thy perfect righteousness,
 And mention none but thine.

Men ought always to pray, and not to faint.
Luke 18:1.

April

16. The beloved of the Lord shall dwell in safety by him, and the Lord shall cover him all the day long.
Deut. 33:12.

As the bird beneath her feathers
 Guards the object of her care,
So the Lord his children gathers,
 Spreads his wings and hides them there;
Thus protected, All their foes they boldly dare.

Keep me as the apple of the eye, hide me under the shadow of thy wings. *Psalm 17:8.*

Daily Food

April

17. Come now, and let us reason together, saith the Lord: though your sins be as scarlet, they shall be as white as snow; though they be red like crimson, they shall be as wool. *Isaiah 1:18.*

For Him who washed you in his blood,
  Ye saints, your loudest songs prepare:
He sought you wandering far from God,
  And now preserves you by his care.

Now, in Christ Jesus, ye who sometime were far off, are made nigh by the blood of Christ. *Eph. 2:13.*

April

18. I had fainted, unless I had believed to see the goodness of the Lord in the land of the living.
Psa. 27:13.

Friend of the friendless and the faint,
  Where shall I lodge my deep complaint?
Where but with thee, whose open door
  Invites the helpless and the poor?

O God, thou art my God; early will I seek thee.
Psalm 63:1.

April

19. The meek shall increase their joy in the Lord.
Isaiah 29:19.

When Christ by faith is present,
 The sinner's troubles cease;
His ways are truly pleasant,
 And all his paths are peace.

The Lord lifteth up the meek: he casteth the wicked down to the ground. *Psalm 147:6.*

April

20. He shall never suffer the righteous to be moved.
Psalm 55:22.

Dear Saviour, let us never be,
 Before the world, ashamed of thee,
 Nor shrink from duty's call:
 Our work to do thee service here,
Our hope in glory to appear,
 Where thou art all in all.

He that is righteous, let him be righteous still; and he that is holy, let him be holy still. *Rev. 22:11.*

Daily Food

April

21. Let not your heart be troubled; ye believe in God, believe also in me. *John 14:1.*

Jesus, hear our humble prayer;
 Tender Shepherd of thy sheep,
Let thy mercy and thy care
 All our souls in safety keep.

The Lord of hosts is with us; the God of Jacob is our refuge. *Psalm 46:11.*

April

22. I wait for the Lord, my soul doth wait, and in his word do I hope. *Psalm 130:5.*

Lord Jesus, help me now to flee
 And seek my hope alone in thee;
Apply thy blood, thy Spirit give,
 Subdue my sin, and let me live.

Bring forth therefore fruits meet for repentance.
Matt. 3:8.

Daily Food

April

23. Rejoice not against me, O mine enemy; when I fall, I shall arise. *Micah 7:8.*

Let the fainting soul be cheerful,
 Let the timid now be brave;
Why should they be faint or fearful,
 Whom the Lord delights to save?
  Whom he rescues,
 Satan can no more enslave.

Lord, lift thou up the light of thy countenance upon us. *Psalm 4:6.*

April

24. Truly my soul waiteth upon God; from him cometh my salvation. *Psalm 62:1.*

Quiet, Lord, my froward heart;
 Make me teachable and mild,
Upright, simple, free from art,
 Like a little weaned child:
From distrust and envy free,
 Pleased with all that pleases thee.

I have waited for thy salvation, O Lord. *Gen. 49:18.*

April

25. Who forgiveth all thine iniquities; who healeth all thy diseases. *Psa. 103:3.*

Thanks for mercies past receive,
 Pardon of our sins renew;
 Teach us henceforth how to live
 With eternity in view.

Bless the Lord, O my soul, and forget not all his benefits. *Psa. 103:2.*

April

26. Let Israel hope in the Lord; for with the Lord there is mercy, and with him is plenteous redemption. *Psalm 130:7.*

There's full redemption at his throne,
 For sinners long enslaved:
 The great Redeemer is his Son,
 And Israel shall be saved.

In whom we have redemption through his blood, the forgiveness of sins, according to the riches of his grace. *Eph. 1:7.*

April

27. Take my yoke upon you, and learn of me; for I am meek and lowly in heart; and ye shall find rest unto your souls. *Matt. 11:29.*

They shall find rest that learn of me,
 I'm of a meek and lowly mind,
But passion rages like the sea,
 And pride is restless as the wind.

Help us, O Lord our God, for we rest on thee.
2 Chron. 14:11.

April

28. Draw nigh to God, and he will draw nigh to you. *James 4:8.*

Come, ye weary, heavy-laden,
 Lost and ruined by the fall;
If you tarry till you're better,
 You will never come at all:
  Not the righteous,
 Sinners Jesus came to call.

It is good for me to draw near to God. *Psalm 73:28.*

April

29. Mercy shall be built up for ever; thy faithfulness shalt thou establish in the very heavens.
Psalm 89:2.

The sacred truths his lips pronounce,
  Shall firm as heaven endure;
And if he speak a promise once,
  The eternal grace is sure.

Let them that suffer according to the will of God, commit the keeping of their souls to him in well-doing, as unto a faithful Creator. *I Pet. 4:19.*

April

30. My yoke is easy, and my burden is light.
Matt. 11:30.

Blest is the man whose shoulders take
  My yoke, and bear it with delight;
My yoke is easy to his neck,
  My grace shall make the burden light.

Her ways are ways of pleasantness, and all her paths are peace. *Prov. 3:17*

Daily Food

May

5 Roses and Bluebells

Daily Food

May

1. The Lord is our judge, the Lord is our lawgiver, the Lord is our king; he will save us.
Isa. 33:22.

Thy throne, O God, for ever stands,
  Grace is the sceptre in thy hands;
Thy laws and words are just and right,
  Justice and grace are thy delight.

Save us, O God of our salvation. *I Chron. 16:35.*

May

2. The grass withereth, the flower fadeth; but the word of our God shall stand for ever. *Isa. 40:8.*

We've no abiding city here;
  This may distress the worldling's mind,
But should not cost the saint a tear,
  Who hopes a better rest to find.

Search the Scriptures, for in them ye think ye have eternal life: and they are they which testify of me.
John 5:39

Daily Food

May

3. Fear thou not, for I am with thee; be not dismayed, for I am thy God. *Isa. 41:10.*

When I walk through the shades of death,
 Thy presence is my stay;
A word of thy supporting breath
 Drives all my fears away.

Lo, I am with you always, even unto the end of the world. *Matt. 28:20.*

May

4. I, even I, am he that blotteth out thy transgressions for mine own sake, and will not remember thy sins. *Isa. 43:25.*

How glorious is that righteousness
 Which cancels the believer's sins;
While a bright evidence of grace
 Through his whole life appears and shines.

Repent ye therefore, and be converted, that your sins may be blotted out. *Acts 3:19.*

Daily Food

May

5. Fear not; for I have redeemed thee, I have called thee by thy name; thou art mine. *Isa. 43:1.*

  The gospel bears my spirit up;
    A faithful and unchanging God
  Lays the foundation of my hope
    In oaths and promises and blood.

Ye were not redeemed with corruptible things, as silver and gold; but with the precious blood of Christ, as of a lamb without blemish and without spot.
I Pet. 1:18, 19.

May

6. I the Lord thy God will hold thy right hand, saying unto thee, Fear not; I will help thee. *Isa. 41:13.*

  Then let our humble faith address
    His mercy and his power;
  We shall obtain delivering grace
    In the distressing hour.

Lord, save me. *Matt. 14:30.*

Daily Food

May

7. The needy shall not always be forgotten.
Psa. 9:18.

When creature comforts fade and die,
 Worldlings may weep, but why should I?
Jesus still lives, and still is nigh.

Ye know the grace of our Lord Jesus Christ, that though he was rich, yet for your sakes he became poor, that ye through his poverty might be rich.
2 Cor. 8:9.

May

8. The expectation of the poor shall not perish for ever. *Psalm 9:18.*

A certain refuge Christ will prove
 For all the poor oppressed;
To save the people of his love,
 And give the weary rest.

This poor man cried, and the Lord heard him, and saved him out of all his troubles.
Psalm 34:6.

Daily Food

May

9. In thy presence is fulness of joy; at thy right hand there are pleasures for evermore.
Psalm 16:11.

What sinners value I resign;
 Lord, 'tis enough, if thou art mine;
I shall behold thy blissful face,
 And stand complete in righteousness.

To me to live is Christ, and to die is gain.
Phil. 1:21.

May

10. The Lord is my rock, and my fortress, and my deliverer. *Psalm 18:2.*

Thee will I love, O Lord, my strength,
 My rock, my tower, my high defence;
Thy mighty arm shall be my trust,
 For I have found salvation thence.

Boast not thyself of to-morrow; for thou knowest not what a day may bring forth.
Prov. 27:1.

Daily Food

May

11. Thou wilt save the afflicted people.
Psalm 18:27.

Just in the last distressing hour
 The Lord displays delivering power;
The mount of danger is the place
 Where we shall see surprising grace.

Lord, save us: we perish.
Matt. 8:25.

May

12. The Lord is my strength.
Hab. 3:19.

Though pressed, we will not yield,
 But shall prevail at length;
Christ is our sun and shield,
 Our righteousness and strength.

Although the fig-tree shall not blossom, neither shall fruit be in the vines; the labor of the olive shall fail, and the fields shall yield no meat; the flock shall be cut off from the fold, and there shall be no herd in the stalls: yet I will rejoice in the Lord, I will joy in the God of my salvation. *Hab. 3:17, 18.*

Daily Food

May

13. I am the light of the world; he that followeth me shall not walk in darkness, but shall have the light of life. *John 8:12.*

Great Sun of righteousness, arise,
 Bless the dark world with heavenly light;
Thy gospel makes the simple wise,
 Thy laws are pure, thy judgments right.

The Lord my God will enlighten my darkness. *Psalm 18:28.*

May

14. He hath not despised nor abhorred the affliction of the afflicted. *Psa. 22:24.*

Afflictions, though they seem severe,
 In mercy oft are sent;
They stopped the prodigal's career,
 And forced him to repent.

Despise not the chastening of the Lord, neither be weary of his correction; for whom the Lord loveth he correcteth, even as a father the son in whom he delighteth. *Prov. 3:11, 12.*

Daily Food

May

15. Who is a God like unto thee, that pardoneth iniquity? *Mic. 7:18.*

O save a trembling sinner, Lord,
 Whose hope, still hovering round thy word,
 Would light on some sweet promise there,
 Some sure support against despair.

Have mercy on us, O Lord, thou Son of David.
Matt. 20:31.

May

16. I am the Lord, I change not; therefore ye sons of Jacob are not consumed. *Mal. 3:6.*

O let me then at length be taught,
 What I am still so slow to learn,
 That God is love, and changes not,
 Nor knows the shadow of a turn.

Every good gift and every perfect gift is from above, and cometh down from the Father of lights, with whom is no variableness, neither shadow of turning.
James 1:17.

Daily Food

May

17. He retaineth not his anger for ever, because he delighteth in mercy.
Miah. 7:18.

Blest is the man to whom the Lord
 Imputes not his iniquities;
He pleads no merit of reward,
 And not on works but grace relies.

For he hath made him to be sin for us, who knew no sin; that we might be made the righteousness of God in him. *2 Cor. 5:21.*

May

18. He will subdue our iniquities; and thou wilt cast all their sins into the depths of the sea.
Micah 7:19.

Our very frame is mixed with sin,
 His spirit makes our nature clean;
Such virtues from his sufferings flow,
 At once to cleanse and pardon too.

Thou shalt call his name Jesus; for he shall save his people from their sins. *Matt. 1:21.*

May

19. The Lord is slow to anger, and great in power, and will not at all acquit the wicked: the Lord hath his way in the whirlwind and in the storm, and the clouds are the dust of his feet. *Nahum 1:3.*

It is the Lord! shall I resist
 Or contradict his will
Who cannot do but what is just,
 And must be righteous still?

Be ye reconciled to God. *2 Cor. 5:20.*

May

20. The Lord is good, a strong-hold in the day of trouble: and he knoweth them that trust in him.
Nah. 1:7.

My Shepherd will supply my need,
 Jehovah is his name;
In pastures fresh he makes me feed,
 Beside the living stream.

I am the good Shepherd, and know my sheep.
John 10:14.

Daily Food

May

21. The earth shall be filled with the knowledge of the glory of the Lord, as the waters cover the sea. *Hab. 2:14.*

Jesus shall reign where'er the sun
  Does his successive journeys run.
His kingdom stretch from shore to shore,
  Till moons shall wax and wane no more.

O Lord, revive thy work in the midst of the years. *Hab. 3:2.*

May

22. The Lord thy God in the midst of thee is mighty; he will save, he will rejoice over thee with joy; he will rest in his love, he will joy over thee with singing. *Zeph. 3:17.*

How can I sink with such a prop
  As my eternal God,
Who bears the earth's huge pillars up,
  And spreads the heavens abroad?

In that day it shall be said to Jerusalem, Fear thou not; and to Zion, Let not thy hands be slack. *Zeph. 3:16.*

Daily Food

May

23. I will pour upon the house of David, and upon the inhabitants of Jerusalem, the Spirit of grace and of supplications: and they shall look upon me whom they have pierced, and they shall mourn.
Zech. 12:10.

Strike, mighty grace, my flinty soul,
 Till melting waters flow,
And deep repentance drown mine eyes
 In undissembled woe.

Rend your heart, and not your garments, and turn unto the Lord your God; for he is gracious and merciful, slow to anger, and of great kindness.
Joel 2:13.

May

24. His mercy is on them that fear him.
Luke 1:50.

In vain the trembling conscience seeks
 Some solid ground to rest upon;
With long despair the spirit breaks,
 Till we apply to Christ alone.

Ye that fear the Lord, trust in the Lord; he is their help and their shield. *Psalm 115:11.*

Daily Food

May

25. There shall be a fountain opened to the house of David, and to the inhabitants of Jerusalem, for sin and for uncleanness. *Zech. 13:1.*

Come, and he'll cleanse our spotted souls,
 And wash away our stains,
In the dear fountain that his Son
 Poured from his dying veins.

Create in me a clean heart, O God, and renew a right spirit within me. *Psalm 51:10.*

May

26. If two of you shall agree on earth, as touching any thing that they shall ask, it shall be done for them. *Matt. 18:19.*

Prayer was appointed to convey
 The blessings God designs to give;
Long as they live should Christians pray,
 For only while they pray they live.

Be careful for nothing; but in every thing by prayer and supplication with thanksgiving let your requests be made known unto God. *Phil. 4:6.*

Daily Food

May

27. Return unto me, and I will return unto you, saith the Lord of hosts. *Mal. 3:7.*

Jesus, we come at thy command,
 With faith and hope and humble zeal
Resign our spirits to thy hand,
 To mould and guide us at thy will.

Him hath God exalted with his right hand to be a Prince and a Saviour, for to give repentance to Israel, and forgiveness of sins. *Acts 5:31.*

May

28. Unto you that fear my name, shall the Sun of righteousness arise with healing in his wings.
Mal. 4:2.

Through all the storms that veil the skies,
 And frown on earthly things,
The Sun of righteousness shall rise
 With healing in his wings.

Let your light so shine before men, that they may see your good works, and glorify your Father which is in heaven. *Matt. 5:16.*

Daily Food

May

29. Verily, verily, I say unto you, he that believeth on me hath everlasting life. *John 6:47.*

Should all the forms that men devise
 Assault my faith with treacherous art,
I'd call them vanity and lies,
 And bind the gospel to my heart.

He that believeth on the Son of God, hath the witness in himself. *1 John 5:10.*

May

30. The Son of man shall come in the glory of his Father, with his angels; and then he shall reward every man according to his works. *Matt. 16:27.*

See the Judge our nature wearing,
 Clothed in majesty divine;
You, who long for his appearing,
 Then shall say, This God is mine:
  Gracious Saviour,
 Own me in that day for thine.

What is a man profited, if he shall gain the whole world, and lose his own soul? *Matt. 16:26.*

Daily Food

May

31. We are all as an unclean thing, and all our righteousnesses are as filthy rags.
Isaiah 64:6.

Let others in the gaudy dress
 Of fancied merit shine,
The Lord shall be my righteousness,
 The Lord for ever mine.

I count all things but loss for the excellency of the knowledge of Christ Jesus my Lord; for whom I have suffered the loss of all things, and do count them but dung, that I may win Christ, and be found in him, not having mine own righteousness, which is of the law, but that which is through the faith of Christ, the righteousness which is of God by faith.
Phil. 3:8, 9.

Daily Food

June

6 Moss, Roses, and Buds.

Daily Food

June

1. I am the bread of life; he that cometh to me shall never hunger, and he that believeth on me shall never thirst. *John 6:35.*

Though all the flocks and herds were dead,
 My soul a famine need not dread,
For Jesus is my living bread.

Lord, evermore give us this bread.
John 6:34.

June

2. He will turn again, he will have compassion upon us. *Micah 7:19.*

Jesus, my God, thy blood alone
 Hath power sufficient to atone;
Thy blood can make me white as snow,
 No Jewish types could cleanse me so.

God was in Christ, reconciling the world unto himself, not imputing their trespasses unto them. *2 Cor. 5:19.*

Daily Food

June

3. Where two or three are gathered together in my name, there am I in the midst of them. *Matt. 18:20.*

Where two or three, with sweet accord,
  Unite to seek and praise the Lord,
"There," says the Saviour, "will I be
  Amid this little company."

Every one that asketh, receiveth. *Luke 11:10.*

June

4. This is a faithful saying, and worthy of all acceptation, that Christ Jesus came into the world to save sinners: of whom I am chief. *I Tim. 1:15.*

Resting on "this faithful saying,"
  We are safe from force and guile;
On our Lord our spirits staying,
  We may look around and smile.

This is a faithful saying, and these things I will that thou affirm constantly, that they which have believed in God might be careful to maintain good works. *Titus 3:8.*

Daily Food

June

5. Blessed are those servants whom the Lord, when he cometh, shall find watching. *Luke 12:37.*

Watch, 'tis your Lord's command,
 And while we speak he's near;
Mark the first signal of his hand,
 And ready all appear.

Be ye therefore ready also; for the Son of man cometh at an hour when ye think not. *Luke 12:40.*

June

6. All things whatsoever ye shall ask in prayer, believing, ye shall receive. *Matt. 21:22.*

Lord, I cannot let thee go,
 Till a blessing thou bestow;
Do not turn away thy face,
 Mine's an urgent, pressing case.

Pray without ceasing. In every thing give thanks; for this is the will of God in Christ Jesus concerning you. *I Thess. 5:17, 18.*

Daily Food

June

7. I will pray the Father, and he shall give you another comforter, that he may abide with you for ever; even the Spirit of truth.
.*John 14:16, 17.*

Come, Holy Spirit, come,
 With energy divine;
And on my poor benighted soul
 With beams of mercy shine.

Walk in the Spirit. *Gal. 5:16.*

June

8. I will not leave you comfortless; I will come to you. *John 14:18.*

While my spirit within me is pressed
 With sorrow, temptation, and fear,
Like John, I would flee to thy breast,
 And pour my complaints in thine ear.

Abide in him; that when he shall appear, we may have confidence, and not be ashamed before him at his coming. *1 John 2:28.*

Daily Food

June

9. If a man love me, he will keep my words; and my Father will love him, and we will come unto him, and make our abode with him. *John 14:23.*

One there is above all others,
 Well deserves the name of Friend;
His is love beyond a brother's,
 Costly, free, and knows no end:
They who once his kindness prove,
 Find it everlasting love.

He that loveth me not, keepeth not my sayings.
John 14:24.

June

10. Peace I leave with you, my peace I give unto you: not as the world giveth, give I unto you.
John 14:27.

Let worldly minds the world pursue,
 It has no charms for me;
Once I admired its trifles too,
 But grace has set me free.

Let not your heart be troubled, neither let it be afraid.
John 14:27.

Daily Food

June

11. If ye abide in me, and my words abide in you, ye shall ask what ye will, and it shall be done unto you. *John 15:7.*

Knowledge and zeal and gifts and talk,
  Unless combined with faith and love,
And witnessed by a gospel walk,
  Will not a true profession prove.

Herein is my Father glorified, that ye bear much fruit; so shall ye be my disciples. *John 15:8.*

June

12. As the Father hath loved me, so have I loved you. *John 15:9.*

O for grace our hearts to soften,
  Teach us, Lord, at length to love;
We, alas, forget too often
  What a friend we have above:
But when home our souls are brought,
  We will love thee as we ought.

Continue ye in my love. *John 15:9.*

Daily Food

June

13. If ye keep my commandments, ye shall abide in my love. *John 15:10.*

Do not I love thee, O my Lord?
  Behold my heart and see;
And turn each cherished idol out
  That dares to rival thee.

Ye have not chosen me, but I have chosen you, and ordained you, that ye should go and bring forth fruit. *John 15:16.*

June

14. Verily, verily, I say unto you, Whatsoever ye shall ask the Father in my name, he will give it you. *John 16:23.*

What various hinderances we meet,
  In coming to a mercy-seat!
Yet who that knows the worth of prayer,
  But wishes to be often there.

Your sins are forgiven you for his name's sake. *1 John 2:12.*

Daily Food

June

15. Ask, and ye shall receive, that your joy may be full. *John 16:24.*

Prayer makes the darkened cloud withdraw;
 Prayer climbs the ladder Jacob saw,
Gives exercise to faith and love,
 Brings every blessing from above.

In the world ye shall have tribulation: but be of good cheer; I have overcome the world. *John 16:33.*

June

16. Being justified by faith, we have peace with God, through our Lord Jesus Christ. *Rom. 5:1.*

Jesus, thy blood and righteousness
 My beauty are, my glorious dress:
 'Midst flaming worlds, in these arrayed,
 With joy shall I lift up my head.

By whom also we have access by faith into this grace wherein we stand, and rejoice in hope of the glory of God. *Rom. 5:2.*

Daily Food

June

17. God will render to every man according to his deeds; to them who, by patient continuance in well-doing, seek for glory and honor and immortality, eternal life. *Rom. 2:7.*

If thou, my Jesus, still be nigh,
  Cheerful I live, and joyful die;
 Secure, when mortal comforts flee,
  To find ten thousand worlds in thee.

This is life eternal, that they might know thee the only true God, and Jesus Christ whom thou hast sent. *John 17:3.*

June

18. Believe on the Lord Jesus Christ, and thou shalt be saved. *Acts 16:31.*

Lord, I retire beneath thy cross,
 By faith at thy dear feet I lie;
 And the keen sword that justice draws,
  Flaming and red, shall pass me by.

I know whom I have believed. *2 Tim. 1:12.*

Daily Food

June

19. God commendeth his love toward us, in that while we were yet sinners, Christ died for us.
Rom. 5:8.

The cross, its burden, O how great!
 No strength but his *could* bear its weight;
No love but his *would* undertake
 To bear it for the sinner's sake.

Much more then, being now justified by his blood, we shall be saved from wrath through him.
Rom. 5:9.

June

20. Be of good courage, and he shall strengthen your heart, all ye that hope in the Lord.
Psalm 31:24.

Ye humble souls, in every strait,
 On God with sacred courage wait;
His hand will life and strength afford,
 Oh ever wait upon the Lord.

Be not afraid, only believe. *Mark 5:36.*

Daily Food

June

21. His anger endureth but a moment; in his favor is life: weeping may endure for a night, but joy cometh in the morning. *Psalm 30:5.*

Since all that I meet
 Shall work for my good,
The bitter is sweet,
 The medicine is food:
Though painful at present,
 'Twill end before long,
And then, O how pleasant
 The conqueror's song.

Hear, O Lord, and have mercy upon me. Lord, be thou my helper. *Psalm 30:10.*

June

22. The Lord is my light and my salvation; whom shall I fear? *Psa. 27:1.*

Why should I shrink at thy command,
 Whose love forbids my fears;
Or tremble at the gracious hand
 That wipes away my tears?

Teach me thy way, O Lord, and lead me in a plain path. *Psalm 27:11.*

Daily Food

June

23. Whosoever believeth on him shall not be ashamed. *Rom. 9:33.*

Ashamed of Jesus! that dear Friend
  On whom my hopes of heaven depend?
No; when I blush, be this my shame,
  That I no more revere his name.

Rejoice in the Lord always; and again I say, rejoice. *Phil. 4:4.*

June

24. If when we were enemies, we were reconciled to God by the death of his Son; much more, being reconciled, we shall be saved by his life. *Rom. 5:10.*

Jesus, my great High-priest,
  Offered his blood and died:
My guilty conscience seeks
  No sacrifice beside:
His powerful blood did once atone,
  And now it pleads before the throne.

Not only so, but we also joy in God through our Lord Jesus Christ, by whom we have now received the atonement. *Rom. 5:11.*

Daily Food

June

25. If God be for us, who can be against us?
Rom. 8:31.

O why should I murmur and grieve,
  Since my Shepherd is always the same:
And has promised he never will leave
  The soul that confides in his name?

Who shall separate us from the love of Christ? Shall tribulation, or distress, or persecution, or famine, or nakedness, or peril, or sword? *Rom. 8:35.*

June

26. The spirit also helpeth our infirmities; for we know not what we should pray for as we ought; but the Spirit itself maketh intercession for us with groanings which cannot be uttered. *Rom. 8:26.*

Come, gracious Spirit, source of love,
  With light and comfort from above;
Be thou our guardian, thou our guide,
  O'er every thought and step preside.

Quench not the Spirit. *I Thess. 5:19*

Daily Food

June

27. If by one man's offence death reigned by one; much more they which receive abundance of grace, and of the gift of righteousness, shall reign in life by one, Jesus Christ. *Rom. 5:17.*

Thou hast redeemed our souls from death,
 Hast set the prisoner free;
Hast made us kings and priests to God,
 And we shall reign with thee.

Being then made free from sin, ye became the servants of righteousness. *Rom. 6:18.*

June

28. The Lord of hosts is with us; the God of Jacob is our refuge. *Psa. 46:7.*

Great God, assist me through the fight,
 Make me triumphant in thy might:
Thou the desponding heart canst raise-
 The victory mine, and thine the praise.

We are more than conquerors, through him that loved us. *Rom. 8:37.*

Daily Food

June

29. Thou art my hiding-place; thou shalt preserve me from trouble; thou shalt compass me about with songs of deliverance. *Psalm 32:7.*

How are thy servants blessed, O Lord,
 How sure is their defence;
Eternal Wisdom is their guide-
 Their help Omnipotence!

Blessed are all they that put their trust in him.
Psalm 2:12.

June

30. We know that all things work together for good to them that love God, to them who are the called according to his purpose. *Rom. 8:28.*

My Saviour, I would freely yield,
 What most I prize, to thee;
Who never hast a good withheld,
 Or wilt withhold from me.

All are yours, and ye are Christ's. *1 Cor. 3:22, 23.*

Daily Food

July

7 Feast of Roses.

Daily Food

July

1. Whosoever shall give you a cup of water to drink in my name, because ye belong to Christ, verily I say unto you, he shall not lose his reward.
Mark 9:41.

Teach us, O Lord, to keep in view
 Thy pattern, and thy steps pursue;
Let alms bestowed, let kindness done,
 Be witnessed by each rolling sun.

Take heed, and beware of covetousness.
Luke 12:15.

July

2. The Lord is the strength of my life; of whom shall I be afraid? *Psa. 27:1.*

O Lord, my best desire fulfil,
 And help me to resign
Life, health, and comfort to thy will,
 And make thy pleasure mine.

Hide not thy face far from me; put not thy servant away in anger. *Psa. 27:9.*

Daily Food

July

3. I will instruct thee, and teach thee in the way which thou shalt go; I will guide thee with mine eye. *Psa. 32:8.*

What shall be my future lot,
  Well I know concerns me not;
 This should set my heart at rest,
  What thy will ordains is best.

This God is our God for ever and ever; he will be our guide, even unto death. *Psalm 48:14.*

July

4. Many sorrows shall be to the wicked; but he that trusteth in the Lord, mercy shall compass him about. *Psalm 32:10.*

 On us thy providence has shone,
  With gentle smiling rays;
 O may our lips and lives make known
  Thy goodness and thy praise.

Be glad in the Lord, and rejoice, ye righteous; and shout for joy, all ye that are upright in heart. *Psa. 32:11.*

Daily Food

July

5. The Lord is nigh unto them that are of a broken heart, and saveth such as be of a contrite spirit. *Psa. 34:18.*

Come, weary souls, with sin distressed,
 Come and accept the promised rest;
The Saviour's gracious call obey,
 And cast your gloomy fears away.

Look upon mine affliction and my pain, and forgive all my sins. *Psa. 25:18.*

July

6. The eyes of the Lord are upon the righteous, and his ears are open unto their cry. *Psalm 34:15.*

What thou shalt to-day provide,
 Let me as a child receive;
What to-morrow may betide,
 Calmly to thy wisdom leave:
'Tis enough that thou wilt care,
 Why should I the burden bear?

Is any among you afflicted? let him pray. Is any merry? let him sing psalms. *James 5:13.*

Daily Food

July

7. Many are the afflictions of the righteous; but the Lord delivereth him out of them all. *Psalm 34:19.*

Yes, 'tis a rough and thorny road
 That leads us to the saints' abode;
But when our Father's house we gain
 'Twill make amends for all our pain.

Wherefore doth a living man complain, a man for the punishment of his sins? *Lam. 3:39.*

July

8. The Lord redeemeth the soul of his servants, and none of them that trust in him shall be desolate. *Psa. 34:22.*

Mourning souls, dry up your tears,
 Banish all your guilty fears;
See your guilt and curse remove,
 Cancelled by redeeming love.

Being justified freely by his grace, through the redemption that is in Christ Jesus. *Rom. 3:24.*

Daily Food

July

9. Thy mercy, O Lord, is in the heavens, and thy faithfulness reacheth unto the clouds. *Psalm 36:5.*

O make but trial of his love;
 Experience will decide,
How blest are they, and only they,
 Who in his truth confide.

God is faithful, by whom ye were called unto the fellowship of his Son Jesus Christ our Lord.
I Cor. 1:9.

July

10. How excellent is thy loving-kindness, O God! therefore the children of men put their trust under the shadow of thy wings. *Psalm 36:7.*

Through all the changing scenes of life,
 In troubles and in joy,
The praises of my God shall still
 My heart and tongue employ.

They shall be abundantly satisfied with the fatness of thy house, and thou shalt make them drink of the river of thy pleasures. *Psalm 36:8.*

July

11. With thee is the fountain of life: in thy light shall we see light. *Psalm 36:9.*

Plenteous grace with thee is found,
 Grace to pardon all our sin;
Let the healing streams abound,
 Make and keep us pure within.

O continue thy loving-kindness unto them that know thee, and thy righteousness to the upright in heart. *Psalm 36:10.*

July

12. It is a faithful saying: For if we be dead with him; we shall also live with him. *2 Tim. 2:11.*

I plead the merits of thy Son,
 Who died for sinners on the tree;
I plead his righteousness alone-
 O put the spotless robe on me.

He died for all, that they which live should not henceforth live unto themselves, but unto him which died for them, and rose again. *2 Cor. 5:15.*

Daily Food

July

13. If we suffer, we shall also reign with him.
2 Tim. 2:12.

Why should I complain
 Of want or distress,
Temptation or pain?
 He told me no less:
The heirs of salvation,
 I know from his word,
Through much tribulation
 Must follow their Lord.

If we deny him, he also will deny us. *2 Tim. 2:12.*

July

14. If we believe not, yet he abideth faithful; he cannot deny himself. *2 Tim. 2:13.*

O my distrustful heart,
 How small thy faith appears;
But greater, Lord, thou art
 Than all my doubts and fears:
Did Jesus once upon me shine,
 Then Jesus is for ever mine.

Be not faithless, but believing. *John 20:27.*

Daily Food

July

15. The foundation of God standeth sure, having this seal, The Lord knoweth them that are his.
2 Tim. 2:19.

It is the Lord, my covenant God-
  Thrice blessed be his name-
Whose gracious promise, sealed with blood,
  Must ever be the same.

Let every one that nameth the name of Christ depart from iniquity. *2 Tim. 2:19.*

July

16. He is able also to save them to the uttermost that come unto God by him, seeing he ever liveth to make intercession for them. *Heb. 7:25.*

Though faint my prayers and cold my love,
  My steadfast hope shall not remove
While Jesus intercedes above.

For such a High-priest became us, who is holy, harmless, undefiled, and separate from sinners.
Heb. 7:26

Daily Food

July

17. The Lord is faithful, who shall establish you, and keep you from evil. *2 Thess. 3:3.*

Let the sweet hope that thou art mine,
 My life and death attend;
Thy presence through my journey shine,
 And crown my journey's end.

Be not weary in well-doing. *2 Thess. 3:13.*

July

18. In that he himself hath suffered, being tempted, he is able to succor them that are tempted. *Heb. 2:18.*

How bitter that cup
 No heart can conceive,
Which he drank quite up,
 That sinners might live:
His way was much rougher
 And darker than mine;
Did Jesus thus suffer,
 And shall I repine?

If any man will come after me, let him deny himself, and take up his cross and follow me. *Matt. 16:24.*

Daily Food

July

19. Fear not, little flock; for it is your Father's good pleasure to give you the kingdom. *Luke 12:32.*

In the floods of tribulation,
  While the billows o'er me roll,
Jesus whispers consolation,
  And supports my fainting soul.

Seek not what ye shall eat, or what ye shall drink, neither be ye of doubtful mind; rather seek ye the kingdom of God, and all these things shall be added unto you. *Luke 12:29, 31.*

July

20. He that believeth on the Son hath everlasting life. *John 3:36.*

No more, my God, I boast no more
  Of all the duties I have done;
I quit the hopes I held before,
  To trust the merits of thy Son.

He that believeth not the Son shall not see life; but the wrath of God abideth on him. *John 3:36.*

July

21. God forbid that I should glory, save in the cross of our Lord Jesus Christ, by whom the world is crucified unto me, and I unto the world.   *Gal. 6:14.*

When I survey the wondrous cross
 On which the Prince of glory died,
My richest gain I count but loss,
 And pour contempt on all my pride.

If ye then be risen with Christ, seek those things which are above.   *Col. 3:1.*

July

22. God so loved the world, that he gave his only begotten Son, that whosoever believeth in him should not perish, but have everlasting life.   *John 3:16.*

I hope for pardon through thy Son,
 For all the crimes which I have done;
O may the grace which pardons me,
 Constrain me to forgive like thee.

Walk in love, as Christ also hath loved us, and hath given himself for us.   *Eph. 5:2.*

Daily Food

July

23. God sent not his Son into the world to condemn the world, but that the world through him might be saved. *John 3:17.*

Jesus, our great High-priest,
  Has full atonement made:
Ye weary spirits, rest;
  Ye mournful souls, be glad.

This is his commandment, that we should believe on the name of his Son Jesus Christ, and love one another. *I John 3:23.*

July

24. He that covereth his sins shall not prosper; but whoso confesseth and forsaketh them shall have mercy. *Prov. 28:13.*

O to grace how great a debtor
  Daily I'm constrained to be;
Let that grace, Lord, like a fetter,
  Bind my wandering heart to thee.

I said, I will confess my transgressions unto the Lord, and thou forgavest the iniquity of my sin. *Psa. 32:5.*

Daily Food

July

25. They have washed their robes, and made them white in the blood of the Lamb; therefore are they before the throne of God. *Rev. 7:14, 15.*

Thy blood, dear Jesus, thine alone
 Hath sovereign virtue to atone;
Here we will rest our only plea,
 When we approach, great God, to thee.

He that keepeth his commandments dwelleth in him, and he in him. And hereby we know that he abideth in us, by the Spirit which he hath given us. *I John 3:24.*

July

26. Now once in the end of the world hath he appeared, to put away sin by the sacrifice of himself. *Heb. 9:26.*

So great, so vast a sacrifice,
 May well my hope revive;
If God's own Son thus bleeds and dies,
 The sinner sure may live.

Ye are bought with a price; therefore glorify God in your body, and in your spirit, which are God's. *I Cor. 6:20.*

Daily Food

July

27. God is our refuge and strength, a very present help in trouble. *Psa. 46:1.*

In the darkest dispensations
  Doth my faithful Lord appear,
With his richest consolations,
  To reanimate and cheer:
Sweet affliction, sweet affliction,
  Thus to bring my Saviour near.

Therefore will not we fear, though the earth be removed, and though the mountains be carried into the midst of the sea. *Psalm 46:2.*

July

28. God is my salvation and my glory: the rock of my strength, and my refuge, is in God. *Psalm 62:7.*

My spirit looks to God alone,
  My rock and refuge is his throne;
In all my fears, in all my straits,
  My soul on his salvation waits.

Trust in him at all times; ye people, pour out your heart before him: God is a refuge for us. *Psalm 62:8.*

Daily Food

July

29. Humble yourselves in the sight of the Lord, and he shall lift you up. *James 4:10.*

Dear Father, if thy lifted rod
 Resolve to scourge us here below,
Still we must lean upon our God,
 Thine arm shall bear us safely through.

God resisteth the proud, but giveth grace unto the humble. *James 4:6.*

July

30. To this man will I look, even to him that is poor and of a contrite spirit. *Isaiah 66:2.*

The humble soul my words revive,
 I bid the mourning sinner live,
Heal all the broken hearts I find,
 And ease the sorrows of the mind.

I say, through the grace given unto me, to every man that is among you, not to think of himself more highly than he ought to think; but to think soberly, according as God hath dealt to every man the measure of faith. *Rom. 12:3.*

Daily Food

July

31. Henceforth there is laid up for me a crown of righteousness, which the Lord, the righteous Judge, shall give me at that day; and not to me only, but unto all them also that love his appearing.
2 Tim. 4:8.

Blessed are the sons of God;
  They are bought with Jesus' blood;
They are ransomed from the grave,
  Life eternal they shall have:
With them numbered may we be,
  Now and through eternity.

The very God of peace sanctify you wholly; and I pray God your whole spirit and soul and body be preserved blameless unto the coming of our Lord Jesus Christ. Faithful is he that calleth you, who also will do it.
I Thess. 5:23, 24.

Daily Food

August

8 Roses and Rosebuds.

Daily Food

August

1. There is no God else besides me; a just God and a Saviour; there is none besides me. *Isaiah 45:21.*

Great God, with reverence we adore
 Thy justice and thy grace;
And on thy faithfulness and power
 Our firm dependence place.

Look unto me, and be ye saved, all the ends of the earth: for I am God, and there is none else. *Isa. 45:22.*

August

2. Behold, I come as a thief. Blessed is he that watcheth and keepeth his garments, lest he walk naked, and they see his shame. *Rev. 16:15.*

Lord, search my thoughts, and try my ways,
 And make my soul sincere;
Then shall I stand before thy face,
 And find acceptance there.

Watch and pray, that ye enter not into temptation. *Matt. 26:41.*

Daily Food

August

3. All the promises of God in him (Christ) are yea, and in him, Amen, unto the glory of God. *2 Cor. 1:20.*

The work which his goodness began,
 The arm of his strength will complete;
His promise is yea, and Amen,
 And never was forfeited yet.

Jesus Christ the same yesterday, and to-day, and for ever. *Heb. 13:8.*

August

4. Behold, I stand at the door and knock: if any man hear my voice, and open the door, I will come in to him, and will sup with him, and he with me. *Rev. 3:20.*

Behold a stranger at the door:
 He gently knocks, has knocked before;
Has waited long, is waiting still;
 You use no other friend so ill.

To him that overcometh will I grant to sit with me in my throne, even as I also overcame, and am set down with my Father in his throne. *Rev. 3:21.*

Daily Food

August

5. The Lord will perfect that which concerneth me. Thy mercy, O Lord, endureth for ever.   *Psalm 138:8.*

His saints what is fitting
 Shall ne'er be denied,
So long as 'tis written,
 The Lord will provide.

Forsake not the work of thine own hands.   *Psalm 138:8.*

August

6. God is able to make all grace abound toward you; that ye, always having all sufficiency in all things, may abound, to every good work.
2 Cor. 9:8.

All needful grace will God bestow,
 And crown that grace with glory too;
He gives us all things, and withholds
 No real good from upright souls.

He which soweth sparingly, shall reap also sparingly; and he which soweth bountifully, shall reap also bountifully.   *2 Cor. 9:6.*

August

7. By grace are ye saved, through faith; and that not of yourselves: it is the gift of God. *Eph. 2:8.*

Grace, 'tis a charming sound,
 Harmonious to the ear;
Heaven with the echo shall resound,
 And all the earth shall hear.

We are his workmanship, created in Christ Jesus unto good works, which God hath before ordained that we should walk in them. *Eph. 2:10.*

August

8. Be thou faithful unto death, and I will give thee a crown of life. *Rev. 2:10.*

Then, Saviour, then my soul receive,
 Transported from this vale to live
And reign with thee above;
 Where faith is sweetly lost in sight,
And hope in full, supreme delight,
 And everlasting love.

Let your moderation be known unto all men. The Lord is at hand. *Phil. 4:5.*

Daily Food

August

9. These things have I written unto you that believe on the name of the Son of God; that ye may know that ye have eternal life, and that ye may believe on the name of the Son of God. *1 John 5:13.*

Faith hath an overcoming power,
 It triumphs in the dying hour;
 Christ is our life, our joy, our hope,
 Nor can we sink with such a prop.

And this is the confidence that we have in him, that if we ask any thing according to his will, he heareth us.
1 John 5:14.

August

10. God hath given to us eternal life; and this life is in his Son. *1 John 5:11.*

How can I die while Jesus lives?
 Who rose and left the dead;
 Pardon and grace my soul receives
 From mine exalted Head.

He that hath the Son, hath life; and he that hath not the Son, hath not life. *1 John 5:12.*

August

11. He that overcometh, the same shall be clothed in white raiment; and I will not blot out his name out of the book of life, but I will confess his name before my Father, and before his angels. *Rev. 3:5.*

In thy fair book of life divine,
 My God, inscribe my name;
There let it fill some humble place
 Beneath my Lord the Lamb.

Be watchful, and strengthen the things which remain, that are ready to die. *Rev. 3:2.*

August

12. In due season we shall reap, if we faint not.
Gal. 6:9.

Though seed lie buried long in dust,
 'Twill not deceive our hope;
The precious grain can ne'er be lost,
 For grace insures the crop.

Let us not be weary in well-doing.
Gal. 6:9.

August

13. Blessed are the dead which die in the Lord.
Rev. 14:13.

Teach me to live, that I may dread
  The grave as little as my bed;
Teach me to die, that so I may
  Rise glorious at the judgment-day.

Yea, saith the Spirit, that they may rest from their labors; and their works do follow them.
Rev. 14:13.

August

14. God is not unrighteous to forget your work and labor of love. *Heb. 6:10.*

True faith unites to Christ the root,
  By him producing holy fruit;
And they who no such fruit can show
  Still on the stock of nature grow.

Be not slothful, but followers of them who through faith and patience inherit the promises.
Heb. 6:12.

August

15. The Lord is gracious, and full of compassion; slow to anger, and of great mercy.
Psalm 145:8.

Come, thou fount of every blessing,
 Tune my heart to sing thy grace;
Streams of mercy, never ceasing,
 Call for songs of loudest praise.

I beseech you therefore, brethren, by the mercies of God, that ye present your bodies a living sacrifice, holy, acceptable unto God, which is your reasonable service. *Rom. 12:1.*

August

16. Return, ye backsliding children, and I will heal your backslidings. *Jer. 3:22.*

Prone to wander, Lord, I feel it,
 Prone to leave the God I love;
Here's my heart, Lord, take and seal it,
 Seal it from thy courts above.

Behold, we come unto thee; for thou art the Lord our God. *Jer. 3:22.*

Daily Food

August

17. Delight thyself also in the Lord, and he shall give thee the desires of thy heart. *Psalm 37:4.*

O Lord, I would delight in thee,
 And on thy care depend;
 To thee in every trouble flee,
 My best, my only friend.

So run, that ye may obtain. *I Cor. 9:24.*

August

18. Commit thy way unto the Lord; trust also in him; and he shall bring it to pass. *Psalm 37:5.*

All my times shall ever be
 Ordered by thy wise decree;
 Times of sickness, times of health,
 Times of penury and wealth,
Times of trial and of grief,
 Times of triumph and relief.

O Lord, I know that the way of man is not in himself: it is not in man that walketh to direct his steps.
Jer. 10:23.

Daily Food

August

19. Our light affliction, which is but for a moment, worketh for us a far more exceeding and eternal weight of glory. *2 Cor. 4:17.*

Trials make the promise sweet,
 Trials give new life to prayer;
Bring me to the Saviour's feet,
 Lay me low and keep me there.

We walk by faith, not by sight.
2 Cor. 5:7.

August

20. Trust in the Lord, and do good; so shalt thou dwell in the land, and verily thou shalt be fed.
Psa. 37:3.

If he shed his precious blood
 To bring me to his fold,
Can I think that any good
 He ever will withhold?

Fret not thyself because of evil-doers, neither be thou envious against the workers of iniquity.
Psa. 37:1.

Daily Food

August

21. To him that ordereth his conversation aright, will I show the salvation of God. *Psalm 50:23.*

Be this my one great business here,
 With holy trembling, holy fear,
To make my calling sure;
 Thine utmost counsel to fulfil,
And suffer all thy righteous will,
 And to the end endure.

Abstain from all appearance of evil. *I Thess. 5:22.*

August

22. Call upon me in the day of trouble: I will deliver thee, and thou shalt glorify me. *Psalm 50:15.*

Dear refuge of my weary soul,
 On thee, when sorrows rise-
 On thee, when waves of trouble roll,
 My fainting hope relies.

O Lord, correct me, but with judgment: not in thine anger, lest thou bring me to nothing.
Jer. 10:24.

Daily Food

August

23. The steps of a good man are ordered by the Lord, and he delighteth in his way: though he fall, he shall not be utterly cast down, because the Lord upholdeth him with his hand. *Psalm 37:23, 24.*

Sovereign Ruler of the skies,
 Ever gracious, ever wise,
All my times are in thy hand,
 All events at thy command.

Walk circumspectly, not as fools, but as wise, redeeming the time. *Eph. 5:15, 16.*

August

24. The salvation of the righteous is of the Lord; he is their strength in the time of trouble.
Psa. 37:39.

Lord, who hast suffered all for me,
 My peace and pardon to procure,
The lighter cross I bear for thee,
 Help me with patience to endure.

Blessed be God, which hath not turned away my prayer, nor his mercy from me. *Psalm 66:20.*

Daily Food

August

25. Thy mercy is great above the heavens, and thy truth reacheth unto the clouds. *Psalm 108:4.*

Approach, my soul, the mercy-seat,
 Where Jesus answers prayer;
There humbly fall before his feet,
 For none can perish there.

Be thou exalted, O God, above the heavens, and thy glory above all the earth. *Psalm 108:5.*

August

26. They that sow in tears shall reap in joy.
Psalm 126:5.

Let those that sow in sadness wait
 Till the fair harvest come;
They shall confess their sheaves are great,
 And shout the blessings home.

He that goeth forth and weepeth, bearing precious seed, shall doubtless come again with rejoicing, bringing his sheaves with him.
Psalm 126:6.

August

27. Through God we shall do valiantly; for he it is that shall tread down our enemies. *Psalm 60:12.*

Let us sing though fierce temptation
 Threaten hard to bear us down;
For the Lord, our strong salvation,
 Holds in view the conqueror's crown.
He that washed us in his blood,
 Soon will bring us home to God.

Thanks be to God, which giveth us the victory, through our Lord Jesus Christ. *1 Cor. 15:57.*

August

28. Thou, Lord, art good, and ready to forgive, and plenteous in mercy unto all them that call upon thee. *Psa. 86:5.*

Mercy, good Lord, mercy I seek.
 This is the total sum;
Mercy, through Christ, is all my suit,
 Lord, let thy mercy come.

Be merciful unto me, O Lord; for I cry unto thee daily. *Psalm 86:3.*

Daily Food

August

29. Though the Lord be high, yet hath he respect unto the lowly. *Psa. 138:6.*

Poor, weak, and worthless though I am,
 I have a rich almighty Friend;
Jesus the Saviour is his name-
 He freely loves, and without end.

Whether therefore ye eat, or drink, or whatsoever ye do, do all to the glory of God. *I Cor. 10:31.*

August

30. Though I walk in the midst of trouble, thou wilt revive me. *Psalm 138:7.*

Though troubles assail,
 And dangers affright;
Though friends should all fail,
 And foes all unite;
Yet one things secures us,
 Whatever betide;
The Scripture assures us,
 The Lord will provide.

Behold, God is my helper. *Psalm 54:4.*

August

31. The Spirit and the bride say, Come. And let him that heareth say, Come. And let him that is athirst come. And whosoever will, let him take the water of life freely. *Rev. 22:17.*

Though his majesty be great,
 His mercy is no less;
 Though he thy transgressions hate,
 He feels for thy distress:
Yield not then to unbelief,
 While he says, There yet is room:
Though of sinners thou art chief,
 Since Jesus calls thee, come.

Be strong in the grace that is in Christ Jesus.
2 Tim. 2:1.

Daily Food

September

9 Roses and Bluebells.

September

1. Yet a little while, and he that shall come will come, and will not tarry.
Heb. 10:37.

If from guilt and sin set free,
 By the knowledge of thy grace,
Welcome then the call will be
 To depart and see thy face.

Ye have need of patience, that after ye have done the will of God, ye might receive the promise.
Heb. 10:36.

September

2. The Lord knoweth how to deliver the godly out of temptations. *2 Pet. 2:9.*

Christ knows how much the weak can bear,
 And helps them when they cry;
The strongest have no strength to spare,
 For such he'll strongly try.

Lead us not into temptation; but deliver us from evil.
Matt. 6:13.

Daily Food

September

3. The just shall live by faith; but if any man draw back, my soul shall have no pleasure in him.
Heb. 10:38.

Grace alone can cure our ills,
  Sweeten life with all its cares,
Regulate our stubborn wills,
  Save us from surrounding snares.

But we are not of them who draw back unto perdition, but of them that believe to the saving of the soul.
Heb. 10:39.

September

4. Call unto me, and I will answer thee, and show thee great and mighty things, which thou knowest not.
Jer. 33:3.

When my prayers are a burden and task,
  No wonder I little receive:
O Lord, make me willing to ask,
  Since thou art so ready to give.

Into thy hand I commit my spirit; thou hast redeemed me, O Lord God of truth.   *Psalm 31:5.*

September

5. The Lord will not cast off for ever; but though he cause grief, yet will he have compassion according to the multitude of his mercies. *Lam. 3:31, 32.*

No voice but thine can give me rest,
 And bid my fears depart;
No love but thine can make me blest,
 And satisfy my heart.

He doth not afflict willingly, nor grieve the children of men. *Lam. 3:33.*

September

6. And I will put my Spirit within you, and cause you to walk in my statutes. *Ezek. 36:27.*

O send thy Spirit down to write
 Thy law upon my heart,
Nor let my tongue indulge deceit,
 Nor act the liar's part.

Help us, O God of our salvation, for the glory of thy name; and deliver us, and purge away our sins, for thy name's sake. *Psalm 79:9.*

September

7. Thou, O Lord, remainest for ever; thy throne from generation to generation. *Lam. 5:19.*

This God is the God we adore,
 Our faithful, unchangeable friend,
Whose love is as great as his power,
 And neither knows measure nor end.

Turn thou us unto thee, O Lord, and we shall be turned. *Lam. 5:21.*

September

8. A new heart also will I give you, and a new spirit will I put within you; and I will take away the stony heart out of your flesh, and I will give you a heart of flesh. *Ezek. 36:26.*

Great God, create my heart anew,
 And form my spirit pure and true;
 O make me wise betimes to spy
 My danger and my remedy.

O remember not against us former iniquities; let thy tender mercies speedily prevent us. *Psalm 79:8.*

September

9. In a little wrath I hid my face from thee for a moment; but with everlasting kindness will I have mercy on thee. *Isa. 54:8.*

God of my life, how good, how wise
 Thy judgments to my soul have been;
They were but mercies in disguise,
 The painful remedies of sin:
How different now thy ways appear,
 Most merciful when most severe.

I will say unto God, Do not condemn me; show me wherefore thou contendest with me. *Job 10:2.*

September

10. Incline your ear, and come unto me: hear, and your souls shall live; and I will make an everlasting covenant with you. *Isa. 55:3.*

Our God will every want supply,
 And fill our hearts with peace;
He gives by covenant and by oath,
 The riches of his grace.

Seek ye the Lord while he may be found, call ye upon him while he is near. *Isa. 55:6.*

Daily Food

September

11. Brethren, give diligence to make your calling and election sure: for if ye do these things, ye shall never fall. *2 Pet. 1:10.*

Though we are feeble, Christ is strong,
 His promises are true;
We shall be conquerors all ere long,
 And more than conquerors too.

For so an entrance shall be ministered unto you abundantly into the everlasting kingdom of our Lord and Saviour Jesus Christ. *2 Pet. 1:11.*

September

12. The Lord hath comforted his people, and will have mercy upon his afflicted. *Isa. 49:13.*

All my trust on thee is stayed,
 All my help from thee I bring:
Cover my defenceless head
 With the shadow of thy wing.

Hear me when I call, O God of my righteousness: thou hast enlarged me when I was in distress; have mercy upon me. *Psalm 4:1.*

Daily Food

September

13. I the Lord am thy Saviour and thy Redeemer.
Isa. 49:26.

Not the labor of my hands
 Can fulfil thy law's demands;
Could my zeal no respite know,
 Could my tears for ever flow,
All for sin could not atone;
 Thou must save, and thou alone.

Lead me, O Lord, in thy righteousness, because of mine enemies; make thy way straight before my face.
Psa. 5:8.

September

14. The Lord God will help me; therefore shall I not be confounded. *Isa. 50:7.*

On thy faithfulness relying,
 We may boldly meet the foe,
All his boasted power defying
 While we come defended so;
  God will save us,
 This our enemies shall know.

Therefore have I set my face like a flint, and I know that I shall not be ashamed. *Isa. 50:7.*

Daily Food

September

15. He is near that justifieth me; who will contend with me? *Isa. 50:8.*

Praise the Lamb – his love unbounded
 Is the theme of praise in heaven;
On his death our hopes are founded,
 For we know his life was given;
And we trust that by his blood
 We are reconciled to God.

Let all those that put their trust in thee rejoice.
Psalm 5:11.

September

16. Behold, the Lord God will help me; who is he that shall condemn me? *Isaiah 50:9.*

Nothing in my hands I bring,
 Simply to thy cross I cling;
Naked, come to thee for dress;
 Helpless, look to thee for grace;
Foul, I to thy fountain fly,
 Wash me, Saviour, or I die.

Preserve me, O God; for in thee do I put my trust
Psalm 16:1.

September

17. I, even I, am he that comforteth you.
Isaiah 51:12.

Shine, Lord, and my terrors shall cease,
 The blood of atonement apply;
And lead me to Jesus for peace,
 The Rock that is higher than I.

Let, I pray thee, thy merciful kindness be for my comfort. *Psa. 119:76.*

September

18. Is Ephraim my dear son? is he a pleasant child? for since I spake against him, I do earnestly remember him still; therefore my bowels are troubled for him: I will surely have mercy upon him, saith the Lord.
Jer. 31:20.

Jesus sought me when a stranger,
 Wandering from the fold of God;
He, to save my soul from danger,
 Interposed his precious blood.

Wilt thou not from this time cry unto me, My Father, thou art the guide of my youth? *Jer. 3:4.*

Daily Food

September

19. All the ends of the earth shall see the salvation of our God. *Isa. 52:10.*

Great God, whose universal sway
  The known and unknown worlds obey,
Now give the kingdom to thy Son,
  Extend his power, exalt his throne.

Pray ye therefore the Lord of the harvest, that he will send forth laborers into his harvest. *Matt. 9:38.*

September

20. He shall see of the travail of his soul, and shall be satisfied: by his knowledge shall my righteous servant justify many; for he shall bear their iniquities. *Isa. 53:11.*

Dear dying Lamb, thy precious blood
  Shall never lose its power,
Till all the ransomed church of God
  Be saved, to sin no more.

As by one man's disobedience many were made sinners, so by the obedience of one shall many be made righteous. *Rom. 5:19.*

September

21. For a small moment have I forsaken thee, but with great mercies will I gather thee.   *Isa. 54:7.*

Good when he gives, supremely good,
  Nor less when he denies:
E'en crosses from his sovereign hand
  Are blessings in disguise.

He will not always chide, neither will he keep his anger for ever.   *Psa. 103:9.*

September

22. All we like sheep have gone astray; we have turned every one to his own way; and the Lord hath laid on him the iniquity of us all.   *Isa. 53:6.*

Let us love and sing and wonder,
  Let us praise the Saviour's name;
He has hushed the law's loud thunder,
  He has quenched mount Sinai's flame:
He has washed us with his blood,
  He has brought us nigh to God.

Ye were as sheep going astray; but are now returned unto the Shepherd and Bishop of your souls.
I Pet. 2:25.

Daily Food

September

23. Ho, every one that thirsteth, come ye to the waters, and he that hath no money; come ye, buy and eat; yea, come, buy wine and milk without money and without price. *Isa. 55:1.*

Ho, ye that pant for living streams,
　And pine away and die;
Here you may quench your raging thirst
　With springs that never dry.

If any man thirst, let him come unto me and drink.
John 7:37.

September

24. All thy children shall be taught of the Lord; and great shall be the peace of thy children. *Isa. 54:13.*

Find in Christ the way of peace,
　Peace unspeakable, unknown;
By his pain he gives you ease,
　Life, by his expiring groan:
Rise, exalted by his fall,
　Find in Christ you all in all.

Great peace have they which love thy law.
Psalm 119:165.

September

25. To the Lord our God belong mercies and forgivenesses, though we have rebelled against him. *Dan. 9:9.*

Jesus, thou art all compassion,
  Pure, unbounded love thou art;
Visit us with thy salvation,
  Enter every trembling heart.

O Lord, to us belongeth confusion of face – because we have sinned against thee. *Dan. 9:8.*

September

26. Rejoice, inasmuch as ye are partakers of Christ's sufferings; that when his glory shall be revealed, ye may be glad also with exceeding joy. *I Pet. 4:13.*

In every pang that rends the heart,
  "The Man of sorrows" had a part;
He sympathizes in our grief,
  And to the sufferer sends relief.

If any man suffer as a Christian, let him not be ashamed, but let him glorify God on this behalf. *I Pet. 4:16.*

Daily Food

September

27. He shall enter into peace: they shall rest in their beds, each one walking in his uprightness.   *Isa. 57:2.*

Lord, it is not life to live,
 If thy presence thou deny;
Lord, if thou thy presence give,
 'Tis no longer death to die:
Source and giver of repose,
 Singly from thy smile it flows;
Peace and happiness are thine-
 Mine they are, if thou art mine.

I shall be satisfied, when I awake, with thy likeness. *Psa. 17:15.*

September

28. I have seen his ways, and will heal him; I will lead him also, and restore comforts unto him and to his mourners.   *Isa. 57:18.*

Cast me not off, almighty Lord,
 But use thy rod and not thy sword.
The cross no longer I decline,
 But save me from the curse divine.

Restore unto me the joy of thy salvation, and uphold me with thy free Spirit.   *Psa. 51:12.*

September

29. I will not contend for ever, neither will I be always wroth; for the spirit should fail before me, and the souls which I have made. *Isa. 57:16.*

My Father in mercy reproves,
  Instructs me by sorrow and smart;
 The veil by correction removes,
  And shows me the ground of my heart.

For the iniquity of his covetousness was I wroth, and smote him. *Isa. 57:17.*

September

30. Peace, peace to him that is far off, and to him that is near, saith the Lord; and I will heal him.
Isa. 57:19.

Give me a calm and thankful heart,
  From every murmur free;
 The blessings of thy grace impart,
  And let me live to thee.

But the wicked are like the troubled sea, when it cannot rest, whose waters cast up mire and dirt. There is no peace, saith my God, to the wicked.
Isa. 57:20, 21.

Daily Food

October

10 Moss, Roses, and Buds.

Daily Food

October

1. The Lord shall be thine everlasting light, and the days of thy mourning shall be ended. *Isa. 60:20.*

In those blest realms of endless day,
  The Lamb shall all our wants supply;
And God's own hand shall wipe away
  The falling tear from every eye.

The city had no need of the sun, neither of the moon, to shine in it; for the glory of God did lighten it, and the Lamb is the light thereof. *Rev. 21:23.*

October

2. It shall come to pass, that before they call, I will answer; and while they are yet speaking, I will hear. *Isa. 65:24.*

Come boldly to the throne of grace,
  Where Jesus kindly pleads;
Ours cannot be a desperate case,
  While Jesus intercedes.

Let us draw near with a true heart, in full assurance of faith. *Heb. 10:22.*

Daily Food

October

3. Behold, thy salvation cometh; behold, his reward is with him, and his work before him. *Isa. 62:11.*

What is it makes my Saviour stay?
  So strong, so ready to redeem?
Not Jesus wills the unkind delay,
  Nor casts out those that come to him:
His grace the secret bar must move,
  Or I shall still reject his love.

He only is my rock and my salvation. *Psa. 62:2.*

October

4. The Lord is nigh unto all them that call upon him, to all that call upon him in truth. *Psa. 145:18.*

He bows his gracious ear,
  We never plead in vain:
Yet we must wait till he appear,
  And pray and pray again.

Unto thee, O Lord, do I lift up my soul.
Psa. 25:1.

Daily Food

October

5. Let your conversation be without covetousness, and be content with such things as ye have; for He hath said, I will never leave thee, nor forsake thee. *Heb. 13:5.*

How well thy blessed truths agree,
 How wise and holy thy commands;
Thy promises how firm they be,
 How firm our hope and comfort stands.

So that we may boldly say, The Lord is my helper, and I will not fear what man shall do unto me. *Heb. 13:6.*

October

6. If any of you lack wisdom, let him ask of God, that giveth to all men liberally, and upbraideth not; and it shall be given him. *Jas. 1:5.*

If pains afflict or wrongs oppress,
 If cares distract or fears dismay,
If guilt deject, if sin distress,
 The remedy's before thee – pray.

But let him ask in faith, nothing wavering. *James 1:6.*

Daily Food

October

7. Israel shall be saved in the Lord with an everlasting salvation.   *Isa. 45:17.*

A debtor to mercy alone,
 Of covenant mercy I sing;
Nor fear, with thy righteousness on,
 My person and offering to bring.

Ye shall not be ashamed nor confounded world without end.   *Isa. 45:17.*

October

8. The mountains shall depart, and the hills be removed; but my kindness shall not depart from thee, neither shall the covenant of my peace be removed, saith the Lord that hath mercy on thee.   *Isaiah 54:10.*

Let the wind blow, and billows roll,
 Hope is the anchor of my soul;
It fastens on a land unknown,
 And moors me to my Father's throne.

Hope maketh not ashamed, because the love of God is shed abroad in our hearts by the Holy Ghost.
Rom. 5:5.

October

9. He was their Saviour: in all their affliction he was afflicted, and the angel of his presence saved them; in his love and in his pity he redeemed them.
Isa. 63:8, 9.

Come boldly to the throne of grace;
  The Saviour's pierced heart
Is touched with our afflicted case
  In its most tender part.
Come boldly to the throne of grace,
  With all your wants and fears;
The Saviour's hand shall kindly chase
  Away the bitterest tears.

He that toucheth you, toucheth the apple of his eye.
Zech. 2:8.

October

10. I said not unto the seed of Jacob, Seek ye me in vain. *Isa. 45:19.*

Ye faithful, hold the promise fast,
  To plead it boldly dare;
Wrestling with God to prove at last
  The omnipotence of prayer.

I the Lord speak righteousness, I declare things that are right. *Isa. 45:19.*

Daily Food

October

11. Blessed are they whose iniquities are forgiven, and whose sins are covered. Blessed is the man to whom the Lord will not impute sin. *Rom. 4:7, 8.*

Nothing but thy blood, O Jesus,
 Can relieve us from our smart;
Nothing else from sin release us,
 Nothing else can melt the heart.
Law and terrors do but harden,
 All the while they work alone;
But a sense of blood-bought pardon
 Soon dissolves a heart of stone.

Who [Jesus our Lord] was delivered for our offences, and was raised again for our justification. *Rom. 4:25.*

October

12. In the Lord shall all the seed of Israel be justified. *Isa. 45:25.*

In thee shall Israel trust,
 And see their guilt forgiven;
God will pronounce the sinner just,
 And take the saint to heaven.

Thou, O Lord, art a shield for me; my glory.
Psalm 3:3.

Daily Food

October

13. He will fulfil the desire of them that fear him: he also will hear their cry, and will save them.
Psa. 145:19.

O sinners, hear his gracious call,
 His mercy's door stands open wide;
He has enough to fill you all,
 And none who come shall be denied.

O my God, I trust in thee; let me not be ashamed, let not mine enemies triumph over me. *Psalm 25:2.*

October

14. I will hear what God the Lord will speak; for he will speak peace unto his people, and to his saints.
Psa. 85:8.

Dread backsliding, scorn dissembling,
 Now salvation's near in view;
Work it out with fear and trembling,
 'Tis your God that works in you.

Work out your own salvation with fear and trembling; for it is God which worketh in you both to will and to do of his good pleasure. *Phil. 2:12, 13.*

Daily Food

October

15. He healeth the broken in heart, and bindeth up their wounds. *Psa. 147:3.*

To humble souls and broken hearts,
 God with his grace is ever nigh;
Pardon and hope his love imparts,
 When men in deep contrition lie.

They that are whole have no need of the physician, but they that are sick. I came not to call the righteous, but sinners, to repentance. *Mark 2:17.*

October

16. Let us hold fast the profession of our faith without wavering; for He is faithful that promised. *Heb. 10:23.*

When my faith is faint and sickly,
 Or when Satan wounds my mind,
Cordials to revive me quickly,
 Healing medicine here I find:
  To the promises I flee,
  Each affords a remedy.

Let us consider one another to provoke unto love and to good works. *Heb. 10:24.*

October

17. He was wounded for our transgressions, he was bruised for our iniquities; the chastisement of our peace was upon him; and with his stripes we are healed. *Isaiah 53:5.*

Weary souls, that wander wide
 From the central point of bliss,
Turn to Jesus crucified,
 Flee to those dear wounds of his.

Who his own self bare our sins in his own body on the tree, that we, being dead to sins, should live unto righteousness. *I Pet. 2:24.*

October

18. It is good for me that I have been afflicted, that I might learn thy statutes. *Psalm 119:71.*

Yes, I have found 'tis good for me
 To bear my Father's rod;
Afflictions make me learn thy law,
 And live upon my God.

Before I was afflicted I went astray; but now have I kept thy word. *Psa. 119:67.*

Daily Food

October

19. Blessed is the man that endureth temptation; for when he is tried, he shall receive the crown of life, which the Lord hath promised to them that love him. *James 1:12.*

Blessed is the man, O God,
  Who stays himself on thee;
Who waits for thy salvation, Lord,
  Shall thy salvation see.

He that endureth to the end shall be saved.
Matt. 10:22.

October

20. Return, thou backsliding Israel, saith the Lord, and I will not cause mine anger to fall upon you; for I am merciful, saith the Lord, and I will not keep anger for ever. *Jer. 3:12.*

Sinners, the voice of God regard,
  'Tis mercy speaks to-day;
He calls you by his sovereign word
  From sin's destructive way.

Only acknowledge thine iniquity, that thou hast transgressed against the Lord thy God. *Jer. 3:13.*

October

21. The Lord is not slack concerning his promise, as some men count slackness; but is long-suffering to us-ward, not willing that any should perish, but that all should come to repentance. *2 Peter 3:9.*

His word of promise is my food,
 His Spirit is my guide;
Thus daily is my strength renewed,
 And all my wants supplied.

Therefore will the Lord wait, that he may be gracious unto you; and therefore will he be exalted, that he may have mercy upon you. *Isa. 30:18.*

October

22. He giveth grace unto the lowly. *Prov. 3:34.*

The more thy glories strike mine eyes,
 The humbler I shall lie;
Thus, while I sink, my joys shall rise
 Immeasurably high.

I abhor myself, and repent in dust and ashes.
Job 42:6.

Daily Food

October

23. Let him that glorieth, glory in this, that he understandeth and knoweth me, that I am the Lord which exercise loving-kindness, judgment, and righteousness in the earth: for in these things I delight, saith the Lord. *Jer. 9:24.*

Nature has all its glories lost
 When brought before his throne;
No flesh shall in his presence boast,
 But in the Lord alone.

Let not the wise man glory in his wisdom, neither let the mighty man glory in his might, let not the rich man glory in his riches. *Jer. 9:23.*

October

24. Thou art my refuge and my portion. *Psalm 142:5.*

'Tis God that lifts our comforts high,
 Or sinks them in the grave;
He gives, and blessed be his name,
 He takes but what he gave.

The Lord gave, and the Lord hath taken away.
Job 1:21.

October

25. Behold what manner of love the Father hath bestowed upon us, that we should be called the sons of God. *I John 3:1.*

> Behold what wondrous grace
>   The Father has bestowed
> On sinners of a mortal race,
>   To call them sons of God.

Beloved, now are we the sons of God, and it doth not yet appear what we shall be; but we know that when he shall appear, we shall be like him; for we shall see him as he is. *I John 3:2.*

October

26. The Lord is good to all, and his tender mercies are over all his works. *Psalm 145:9.*

> Creatures with all their endless race,
>   Thy power and praise proclaim;
> But saints that taste thy richer grace,
>   Delight to bless thy name.

Let every thing that hath breath praise the Lord.
Psalm 150:6.

October

27. I will come again and receive you unto myself; that where I am, there ye may be also.   *John 14:3.*

Though rough and thorny be the road,
  It leads the Christian home to God;
Then count thy present trials small,
  For heaven will make amends for all.

Let us lay aside every weight, and the sin which doth so easily beset us; and let us run with patience the race that is set before us, looking unto Jesus, the author and finisher of our faith.   *Heb. 12:1, 2.*

October

28. He keepeth the paths of judgment, and preserveth the way of his saints.   *Prov. 2:8.*

Make me to walk in thy commands,
  'Tis a delightful road;
Nor let my head, or heart, or hands
  Offend against my God.

I will run the way of thy commandments, when thou shalt enlarge my heart.   *Psalm 119:32.*

October

29. Being justified by faith, we have peace with God, through our Lord Jesus Christ. *Rom. 5:1.*

To see the law by Christ fulfilled,
  And hear his pardoning voice,
Changes a slave into a child,
  And duty into choice.

By whom also we have access by faith into this grace wherein we stand, and rejoice in hope of the glory of God. *Rom. 5:2.*

October

30. I will strengthen thee; yea, I will help thee; yea, I will uphold thee with the right hand of my righteousness. *Isa. 41:10.*

Jesus, how glorious is thy grace,
  When in thy name we trust,
Our faith receives a righteousness
  That makes the sinner just.

Whosoever doeth not righteousness is not of God, neither he that loveth not his brother.
I John 3:10.

October

31. I am not ashamed of the gospel of Christ; for it is the power of God unto salvation to every one that believeth. *Rom. 1:16.*

Ashamed of Jesus! yes, I may,
  When I've no guilt to wash away,
No tear to wipe, no good to crave,
  No fears to quell, no soul to save.

Till then – nor is my boasting vain –
  Till then, I boast a Saviour slain;
And Oh, may this my glory be,
  That Christ is not ashamed of me.

Whosoever shall be ashamed of me and of my words, of him shall the Son of man be ashamed, when he shall come in his own glory, and in his Father's, and of the holy angels. *Luke 9:26.*

Daily Food

November

11 Feast of Roses.

Daily Food

November

1. Thou, Lord, wilt bless the righteous; with favor wilt thou compass him as with a shield.   *Psalm 5:12.*

O may thy Spirit guide my feet
 In ways of righteousness;
Make every path of duty straight,
 And plain before my face.

He that walketh uprightly, walketh surely; but he that perverteth his ways shall be known.   *Prov. 10:9.*

November

2. Behold, I lay in Zion a chief corner-stone, elect, precious: and he that believeth on him shall not be confounded.   *I Peter 2:6.*

Behold the sure foundation-stone
 Which God in Zion lays,
To build our heavenly hopes upon,
 And his eternal praise.

Unto you therefore which believe, he is precious.
I Peter 2:7.

Daily Food

November

3. Comfort ye, comfort ye my people, saith your God; speak ye comfortably to Jerusalem.
Isa. 40:1, 2.

Man may trouble and distress me,
 'Twill but drive me to thy breast;
Life with trials hard may press me,
 Heaven will bring me sweeter rest.
Oh, 'tis not in grief to harm me,
 While thy love is left to me;
Oh, 'twere not in joy to charm me,
 Were that joy apart from thee.

And cry unto her, that her warfare is accomplished, that her iniquity is pardoned. *Isa. 40:2.*

November

4. Surely goodness and mercy shall follow me all the days of my life. *Psa. 23:6.*

The sure provisions of my God
 Attend me all my days;
O may thy house be mine abode,
 And all my work be praise.

And I will dwell in the house of the Lord for ever.
Psalm 23:6.

November

5. As the heaven is high above the earth, so great is his mercy towards them that fear him.
Psalm 103:11.

High as the heavens are raised
  Above the ground we tread,
So far the riches of his grace
  Our highest thoughts exceed.

Show us thy mercy, O Lord, and grant us thy salvation. *Psalm 85:7.*

November

6. As far as the east is from the west, so far hath he removed our transgressions from us. *Psa. 103:12.*

His power subdues our sins;
  And his forgiving love,
Far as the east is from the west,
  Doth all our guilt remove.

Iniquities prevail against me; as for our transgressions, thou shalt purge them away.
Psalm 65:3.

November

7. I will give unto him that is athirst of the fountain of the water of life freely. *Rev. 21:6.*

Life, like a fountain rich and free,
 Springs from the presence of the Lord;
And in thy light our souls shall see
 The blessings promised in thy word.

Keep thy heart with all diligence; for out of it are the issues of life. *Prov. 4:23.*

November

8. Whosoever drinketh of the water that I shall give him shall never thirst; but the water that I shall give him shall be in him a well of water springing up into everlasting life. *John 4:14.*

See, the streams of living waters,
 Springing from eternal love,
Well supply thy sons and daughters,
 And all fear of want remove.

Give me this water, that I thirst not. *John 4:15.*

Daily Food

November

9. Fear not; I am thy shield, and thy exceeding great reward. *Gen. 15:1.*

God is our sun and shield,
 Our light and our defence;
With gifts his hands are filled,
 We draw our blessings thence:
　He shall bestow
　On Jacob's race
　Peculiar grace,
　And glory too.

He that cometh to God must believe that he is, and that he is a rewarder of them that diligently seek him. *Heb. 11:6.*

November

10. The blessing of the Lord, it maketh rich, and he addeth no sorrow with it. *Prov. 10:22.*

No; 'tis in vain to seek for bliss,
 For bliss can ne'er be found,
Till we arrive where Jesus is,
 And tread on heavenly ground.

I will not let thee go, except thou bless me. *Gen. 32:26.*

November

11. Godliness is profitable unto all things, having promise of the life that now is, and of that which is to come. *I Tim. 4:8.*

From covetous desires set free,
 On Jesus cast thy care;
In heaven thy better portion see,
 And let thy heart be there.

Godliness with contentment is great gain. *I Tim. 6:6.*

November

12. The angel of the Lord encampeth round about them that fear him, and delivereth them. *Psalm 34:7.*

He bids his angels pitch their tents
 Round where his children dwell;
What ills their heavenly care prevents,
 No earthly tongue can tell.

Are they not all ministering spirits, sent forth to minister for them who shall be heirs of salvation? *Heb. 1:14.*

Daily Food

November

13. I have loved thee with an everlasting love; therefore with loving-kindness have I drawn thee.
Jer. 31:3.

O love divine, how sweet thou art!
　When shall I find my willing heart
　All taken up by thee?
　I thirst and faint, and die to prove
The greatness of redeeming love,
　The love of Christ to me.

And to know the love of Christ, which passeth knowledge. *Eph. 3:19.*

November

14. I will put my law in their inward parts, and write it in their hearts; and will be their God, and they shall be my people. *Jer. 31:33.*

O how I love thy holy law;
　'Tis daily my delight;
And thence my meditations draw
　Divine advice by night.

O how I love thy law! it is my meditation all the day.
Psalm 119:97.

Daily Food

November

15. The secret of the Lord is with them that fear him, and he will show them his covenant.   *Psalm 25:14.*

The Lord shall make him know
　The secrets of his heart;
The wonders of his covenant show,
　And all his love impart.

Henceforth I call you not servants; for the servant knoweth not what his lord doeth: but I have called you friends; for all things that I have heard of my Father, I have made known unto you.
John 15:15.

November

16. Thy maker is thy husband; the Lord of hosts is his name; and thy Redeemer the Holy One of Israel. *Isa. 54:5.*

Thou dear Redeemer, dying Lamb,
　We love to hear of thee;
No music like thy charming name
　Nor half so sweet can be.

Thou wast slain, and hast redeemed us to God by thy blood.   *Rev. 5:9.*

Daily Food

November

17. The God of peace shall bruise Satan under your feet shortly. *Rom. 16:20.*

Now let my soul arise,
  And tread the tempter down;
My Captain leads me forth
  To conquest and a crown:
A feeble saint shall win the day,
  Though death and hell obstruct the way.

Be sober, be vigilant; because your adversary the devil, as a roaring lion, walketh about, seeking whom he may devour; whom resist steadfast in the faith. *I Peter 5:8, 9.*

November

18. The Lord will give strength unto his people; the Lord will bless his people with peace. *Psalm 29:11.*

The saints shall flourish in his days,
  Dressed in the robes of joy and praise;
Peace, like a river from his throne,
  Shall flow to nations yet unknown.

Mark the perfect man, and behold the upright; for the end of that man is peace. *Psalm 37:37.*

Daily Food

November

19. He that overcometh shall inherit all things; and I will be his God, and he shall be my son.   *Rev. 21:7.*

My dear almighty Lord,
  My Conqueror and my King.
 Thy sceptre and thy sword,
  Thy reigning grace I sing:
Thine is the power; behold, I sit.
  In willing bonds beneath thy feet.

And if a son, then an heir of God through Christ.
Gal. 4:7.

November

20. As one whom his mother comforteth, so will I comfort you.   *Isa. 66:13.*

 O that I could, with favored John
  Recline my weary head upon
 The dear Redeemer's breast!
  From care and sin and sorrow free,
Give me, O Lord, to find in thee
  My everlasting rest.

Blessed be God, even the Father of our Lord Jesus Christ, the Father of mercies, and the God of all comfort, who comforteth us in all our tribulation.
2 Cor. 1:3, 4.

Daily Food

November

21. The Lord taketh pleasure in his people; he will beautify the meek with salvation. *Psalm 149:4.*

The Lord takes pleasure in the just,
 Whom sinners treat with scorn;
The meek, that lie despised in dust,
 Salvation shall adorn.

They shall be mine, saith the Lord of hosts, in that day when I make up my jewels. *Mal. 3:17.*

November

22. This is the promise that he hath promised us, even eternal life. *I John 2:25.*

Nor death, nor hell, shall e'er remove
 His favorites from his breast;
In the dear bosom of his love
 They shall for ever rest.

This is life eternal, that they might know thee the only true God, and Jesus Christ whom thou hast sent. *John 17:3.*

November

23. Thy people shall be willing in the day of thy power. *Psa. 110:3.*

"Come to me," the Saviour cries;
 "Lord, I come," my heart replies;
"Speak the word, and it is done;
 Draw me, Lord, and I shall run."

No man can come to me, except the Father which hath sent me draw him; and I will raise him up at the last day. *John 6:44.*

November

24. He shall cover thee with his feathers, and under his wings shalt thou trust; his truth shall be thy shield and buckler. *Psalm 91:4.*

He that hath made his refuge God,
 Shall find a most secure abode;
Shall walk all day beneath his shade,
 And there at night shall rest his head.

I will say of the Lord, He is my refuge and my fortress: my God; in him will I trust. *Psalm 91:2.*

Daily Food

November

25. I will ransom them from the power of the grave, I will redeem them from death: O death, I will be thy plagues; O grave, I will be thy destruction.
Hosea 13:14.

Say, Live for ever, wondrous King,
  Born to redeem and strong to save;
Then ask the monster, Where's thy sting?
  And where's thy victory, boasting grave?

Death is swallowed up in victory. O death, where is thy sting? O grave, where is thy victory?
I Cor. 15:54, 55.

November

26. Precious in the sight of the Lord is the death of his saints. *Psa. 116:15.*

The graves of all his saints he blessed,
  And softened every bed;
Where should the dying members rest,
  But with the dying Head?

Them also which sleep in Jesus will God bring with him. *I Thess. 4:14.*

Daily Food

November

27. Our God is the God of salvation; and unto God the Lord belong the issues from death.   *Psa. 68:20.*

Our Saviour, Advocate, and Friend,
 On thee our lives and souls depend;
The keys of death and worlds unseen
 Firm in thy hands have ever been:
Thy pierced hands our feet shall lead
 Safe in thy steps through death's dark shade.

I am he that liveth, and was dead; and behold, I am alive for evermore, Amen; and have the keys of hell and of death.   *Rev. 1:18.*

November

28. My mercy will I keep for him for evermore, and my covenant shall stand fast with him.   *Psa. 89:28.*

For ever shall my song record
 The truth and mercy of the Lord;
Mercy and truth for ever stand
 Like heaven, established by his hand.

Thou art my Father, my God, and the Rock of my salvation.   *Psa. 89:26.*

Daily Food

November

29. The Lord hath set apart him that is godly for himself. *Psa. 4:3.*

Know that the Lord divides his saints
 From all the tribes of men beside:
He hears the cries of penitents,
 For the dear sake of Christ that died.

The Lord will hear when I call unto him. Stand in awe, and sin not; commune with your own heart upon your bed, and be still. *Psalm 4:3, 4.*

November

30. The peace of God, which passeth all understanding, shall keep your hearts and minds through Christ Jesus. *Phil. 4:7.*

O Lord, the pilot's part perform,
 And guide and guard me through the storm:
Defend me from each threatening ill;
 Control the waves; say, "Peace, be still."

Now the Lord of peace himself give you peace always by all means. The Lord be with you all.
2 Thess. 3:16.

Daily Food

December

12 Roses and Rosebuds.

Daily Food

December

1. The eyes of the Lord are over the righteous, and his ears are open unto their prayers. *I Pet. 3:12.*

My God, if thou art mine indeed,
  Then I have all my heart can crave;
A present help in time of need,
  Still kind to hear, and strong to save.

But the face of the Lord is against them that do evil.
I Peter 3:12.

December

2. God is not a man, that he should lie; neither the son of man, that he should repent: hath he said, and shall he not do it? or hath he spoken, and shall he not make it good? *Num. 23:19.*

His very word of grace is strong
  As that which built the skies;
The voice that rolls the stars along,
  Speaks all the promises.

Heaven and earth shall pass away, but my words shall not pass away. *Matt. 24:35.*

Daily Food

December

3. That whosoever believeth in him ["the Son of man"] should not perish, but have eternal life.
John 3:15.

Sinners, believe the Saviour's word,
 Trust in his mighty name and live;
A thousand joys his lips afford,
 His hands a thousand blessings give.

He that believeth on him, is not condemned: but he that believeth not, is condemned already, because he hath not believed in the name of the only begotten Son of God. *John 3:18.*

December

4. Unto the upright there ariseth light in the darkness.
Psalm 112:4.

His soul, well fixed upon the Lord,
 Draws heavenly courage from his word;
Amidst the darkness light shall rise,
 To cheer his heart and bless his eyes.

Surely he shall not be moved for ever; the righteous shall be in everlasting remembrance. *Psalm 112:6.*

Daily Food

December

5. They that be wise shall shine as the brightness of the firmament; and they that turn many to righteousness, as the stars for ever and ever. *Dan. 12:3.*

Bright as the firmament above
 The truly wise shall shine,
Reflecting beams of truth and love
 From Christ, their Sun divine.

Then shall the righteous shine forth as the sun in the kingdom of their Father. *Matt. 13:43.*

December

6. The Lord loveth judgment, and forsaketh not his saints; they are preserved for ever. *Psalm 37:28.*

When sinners fall, the righteous stand
 Preserved from every snare;
They shall possess the promised land,
 And dwell for ever there.

Let thy loving-kindness and thy truth continually preserve me. *Psa. 40:11.*

December

7. The steps of a good man are ordered by the Lord; and he delighteth in his way. *Psalm 37:23.*

My God, the steps of pious men
 Are ordered by thy will;
Though they should fall, they rise again,
 Thy hand supports them still.

Make me to go in the path of thy commandments, for therein do I delight. *Psalm 119:35.*

December

8. In the fear of the Lord is strong confidence; and his children shall have a place of refuge.
Prov. 14:26.

Fear him, ye saints, and ye shall then
 Have nothing else to fear;
Make you his service your delight,
 Your wants shall be his care.

The fear of the Lord is a fountain of life.
Prov. 14:27.

Daily Food

December

9. My people shall be satisfied with my goodness, saith the Lord. *Jer. 31:14.*

Thy presence, Lord, can cheer my heart,
 Though every earthly comfort die;
Thy smile can bid my pains depart,
 And raise my sacred pleasures high.

O satisfy us early with thy mercy, that we may rejoice and be glad all our days. *Psalm 90:14.*

December

10. Our Saviour Jesus Christ hath abolished death, and hath brought life and immortality to light through the gospel. *2 Tim. 1:10.*

Firm as his throne his promise stands,
 And he can well secure
What I've committed to his hands
 Till the decisive hour.

I am persuaded that he is able to keep that which I have committed unto him against that day.
2 Tim. 1:12

Daily Food

December

11. He will be very gracious unto thee at the voice of thy cry; when he shall hear it, he will answer thee. *Isaiah 30:19.*

To God I cried when troubles rose,
 He heard me and subdued my foes;
 He did my rising fears control,
 And strength diffused through all my soul.

Quicken us, and we will call upon thy name.
Psalm 80:18.

December

12. The Lord is thy keeper; the Lord is thy shade upon thy right hand. *Psalm 121:5.*

He will sustain our weakest powers
 With his almighty arm;
 And watch our most unguarded hours
 Against surprising harm.

My help cometh from the Lord, who made heaven and earth. *Psa. 121:2.*

Daily Food

December

13. The same Lord over all, is rich unto all that call upon him. *Rom. 10:12.*

O thou, from whom all goodness flows,
  I lift my heart to thee;
In all my sorrows, conflicts, woes,
  Dear Lord, remember me.

For whosoever shall call upon the name of the Lord shall be saved. *Rom. 10:13.*

December

14. Blessed is he that considereth the poor; the Lord will deliver him in time of trouble. *Psalm 41:1.*

Blest is the man whose feelings move
  And melt with pity to the poor,
Whose soul with sympathizing love
  Feels what his fellow-saints endure.

Lord, be merciful unto me; heal my soul, for I have sinned against thee. *Psalm 41:4.*

Daily Food

December

15. The Lord shall preserve thee from all evil; he shall preserve thy soul. *Psa. 121:7.*

He guards thy soul, he keeps thy breath,
  Where thickest dangers come;
Go and return, secure from death,
  Till God commands thee home.

The Lord shall preserve thy going out and thy coming in, from this time forth, and even for evermore. *Psa. 121:8.*

December

16. Ye shall seek me and find me, when ye shall search for me with all your heart. *Jer. 29:13.*

With my whole heart I've sought thy face,
  O let me never stray
From thy commands, O God of grace,
  Nor tread the sinner's way.

With my whole heart have I sought thee; O let me not wander from thy commandments. *Psalm 119:10.*

December

17. As the earth bringeth forth her bud, and as the garden causeth the things that are sown in it to spring forth; so the Lord God will cause righteousness and praise to spring forth before all the nations.
Isaiah 61:11.

O child of sorrow, be it thine to know
  That Scripture only is the cure of woe;
The field of promise, how it flings abroad
  Its perfume o'er the Christian's thorny road;
The soul, reposing on assured relief,
  Feels herself happy amidst all her grief;
Forgets her labors as she toils along,
  Weeps tears of joy, and bursts into a song.

I will greatly rejoice in the Lord, my soul shall be joyful in my God; for he hath clothed me with the garments of salvation, he hath covered me with the robe of righteousness, as a bridegroom decketh himself with ornaments, and as a bride adorneth herself with her jewels.
Isa. 61:10.

December

18. God, willing more abundantly to show unto the heirs of promise the immutability of his counsel, confirmed it by an oath: that by two immutable things, in which it was impossible for God to lie, we might have a strong consolation, who have fled for refuge to lay hold upon the hope set before us.
Heb. 6:17, 18.

How firm a foundation, ye saints of the Lord,
 Is laid for your faith in his excellent word;
 What more can he say, than to you he hath said,
 You who unto Jesus for refuge have fled?

Which hope we have as an anchor of the soul, both sure and steadfast, and which entereth into that within the veil; whither the forerunner is for us entered, even Jesus.
Heb. 6:19, 20.

Daily Food

December

19. The Lord shall be unto thee an everlasting light, and thy God thy glory. *Isaiah 60:19.*

Christ, whose glory fills the skies;
 Christ, the true, the only light,
Sun of righteousness, arise,
 Triumph o'er the shades of night:
Day-spring from on high, be near;
 Day-star in my heart appear.

God be merciful unto us, and bless us, and cause his face to shine upon us. *Psalm 67:1.*

December

20. I have set the Lord always before me: because he is at my right hand, I shall not be moved. *Psa. 16:8.*

My soul would all her thoughts approve
 To his all-seeing eye;
Nor death nor hell my hope shall move,
 While such a friend is nigh.

Therefore my heart is glad, and my glory rejoiceth; my flesh also shall rest in hope. *Psalm 16:9.*

Daily Food

December

21. I will pour my Spirit upon thy seed, and my blessing upon thine offspring: and they shall spring up as among the grass, as willows by the watercourses. *Isaiah 44:3, 4.*

The Holy Spirit must reveal
 The Saviour's work and worth;
Then the hard heart begins to feel
 A new and heavenly birth.

One shall say, I am the Lord's; and another shall call himself by the name of Jacob; and another shall subscribe with his hand unto the Lord, and surname himself by the name of Israel. *Isaiah 44:5.*

December

22. The Lord preserveth all them that love him.
Psalm 145:20.

'Tis Jesus, the first and the last,
 Whose Spirit shall guide us safe home;
We'll praise him for all that is past,
 And trust him for all that's to come.

Let all flesh bless his holy name for ever.
Psalm 145:21.

Daily Food

December

23. Let the wicked forsake his way, and the unrighteous man his thoughts; and let him return unto the Lord, and he will have mercy upon him; and to our God, for he will abundantly pardon.   *Isaiah 55:7.*

Jesus, to thy wounds I fly,
  Purge my sins of deepest dye;
Lamb of God, for sinners slain,
  Wash away my crimson stain.

Thy sins are forgiven.   *Luke 7:48.*

December

24. Christ died for us, that whether we wake or sleep, we should live together with him.   *I Thess. 5:10.*

When from the dust of death I rise
  To take my mansion in the skies,
E'en then shall this be all my plea,
  Jesus hath lived, hath died for me.

Lord Jesus, receive my spirit.   *Acts 7:59.*

Daily Food

December

25. CHRISTMAS-DAY. Unto us a child is born, unto us a son is given: and the government shall be upon his shoulder: and his name shall be called Wonderful, Counsellor, The mighty God, The everlasting Father, The Prince of Peace. Of the increase of his government and peace there shall be no end.
Isa. 9:6, 7.

Hosannah to King David's Son,
 Who reigns on a superior throne!
We bless the Prince of heavenly birth,
 Who brings salvation down to earth.

Let every nation, every age,
 In this delightful work engage:
Old men and babes in Zion sing
 The glowing glories of her King.

Glory to God in the highest, and on earth peace, good-will towards men.
Luke 2:14.

Daily Food

December

26. The Lord hath anointed me to preach good tidings unto the meek; he hath sent me to bind up the broken-hearted, to proclaim liberty to the captives, and the opening of the prison to them that are bound.
Isa. 61:1.

  Jesus, lover of my soul,
    Let me to thy bosom fly,
  While the raging billows roll,
    While the tempest still is nigh.

Hide me, O my Saviour, hide,
    Till the storm of life is past;
Safe into the haven guide,
    O receive my soul at last.

To proclaim the acceptable year of the Lord, and the day of vengeance of our God; to comfort all that mourn; to appoint unto them that mourn in Zion, to give unto them beauty for ashes, the oil of joy for mourning, the garment of praise for the spirit of heaviness.
Isaiah 61:2, 3.

December

27. He hath poured out his soul unto death: and he was numbered with the transgressors; and he bare the sin of many, and made intercession for the transgressors. *Isaiah 53:12.*

Proclaim inimitable love-
 Jesus, the Lord of worlds above,
 Puts off the beams of bright array,
  And veils the God in mortal clay;
He that distributes crowns and thrones,
 Hangs on a tree, and bleeds, and groans;
The Prince of Life resigns his breath,
 The King of Glory bows to death.

Who is he that condemneth? It is Christ that died, yea, rather, that is risen again, who is even at the right hand of God, who also maketh intercession for us. *Rom. 8:34.*

December

28. As the rain cometh down, and the snow from heaven, and returneth not thither, but watereth the earth, and maketh it bring forth and bud, that it may give seed to the sower, and bread to the eater; so shall my word be that goeth forth out of my mouth: it shall not return unto me void, but it shall accomplish that which I please, and it shall prosper in the thing whereto I sent it.
Isa. 55:10, 11.

As rain on meadows newly mown,
 So shall he send his influence down;
His grace on fainting souls distils,
 Like heavenly dew on thirsty hills.

My doctrine shall drop as the rain, my speech shall distil as the dew, as the small rain upon the tender herb, and as the showers upon the grass.
Deut. 32:2.

December

29. The redeemed of the Lord shall return, and come with singing unto Zion, and everlasting joy shall be upon their head; they shall obtain gladness and joy, and sorrow and mourning shall flee away.
Isa. 51:11.

  Cease, ye pilgrims, cease to mourn,
    Press onward to the prize;
  Soon the Saviour will return
    Triumphant in the skies:
Yet a season, and you know
    Happy entrance shall be given;
All your sorrows left below,
    And earth exchanged for heaven.

God shall wipe away all tears from their eyes: and there shall be no more death, neither sorrow, nor crying, neither shall there be any more pain: for the former things are passed away. And he that sat upon the throne said, Behold, I make all things new.
Rev. 21:4, 5.

Daily Food

December

30. Behold, I come quickly; and my reward is with me. *Rev. 22:12.*

A few more rolling suns, at most,
  Will land me on fair Canaan's coast;
Then I shall sing the song of grace,
  And see my Saviour face to face.

Prepare to meet thy God. *Amos 4:12.*

December

31. Surely I come quickly. *Rev. 22:20.*

Lo, he beckons from on high!
  Fearless to his presence fly;
Thine the merit of his blood,
  Thine the righteousness of God:
Angels, joyful to attend,
  Hovering round thy pillow bend,
Wait to catch the signal given,
  And escort thee quick to heaven.

Amen. Even so, come, Lord Jesus. *Rev. 22:20.*

Appendix

This section includes photographs of the original, miniature copy of "Daily Food for Christians."

In order to avoid any damage or overuse of the vintage book, I photographed every single page. I then printed these out and used them as a guide to carefully type every word into this current edition.

Daily Food

Miniature copy of "Daily Food."

Signature and date of original owner. [Oct. 8, 1868]

Daily Food

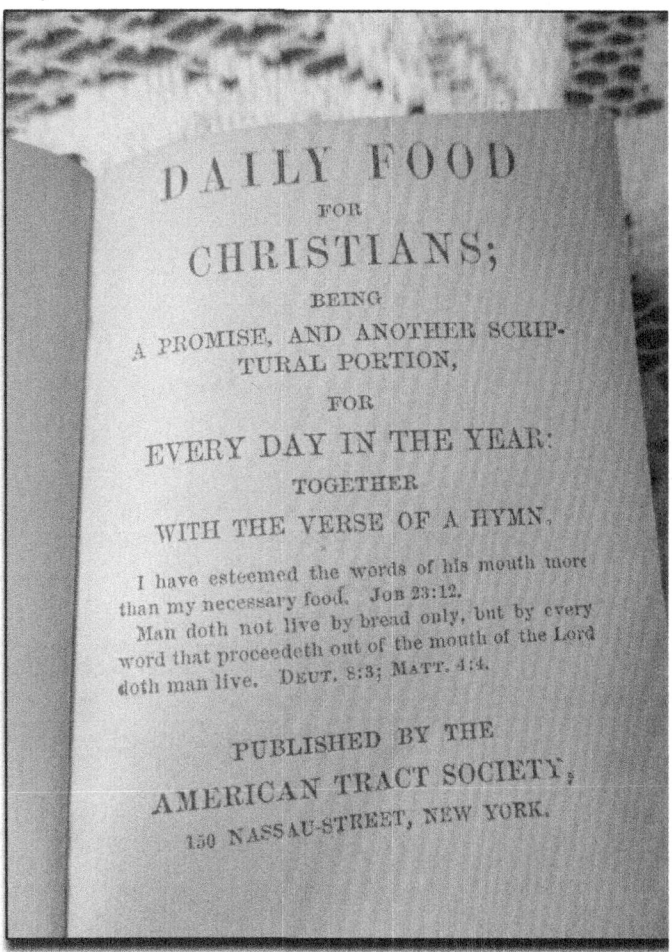

Title page of "Daily Food."

Daily Food

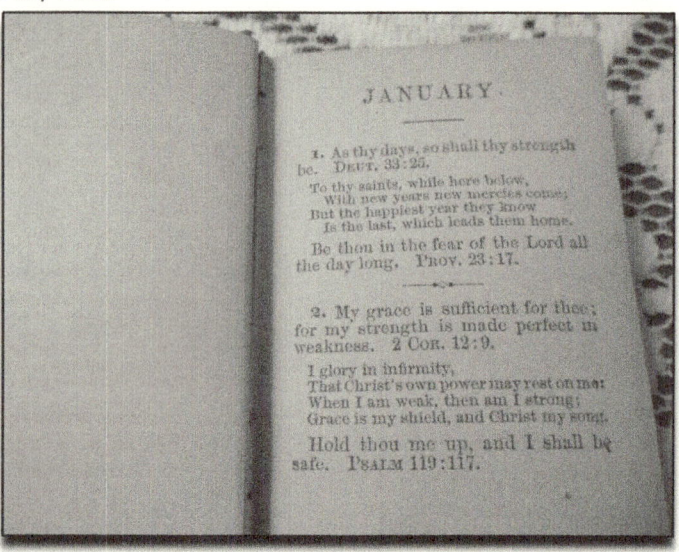

Sample page from January.

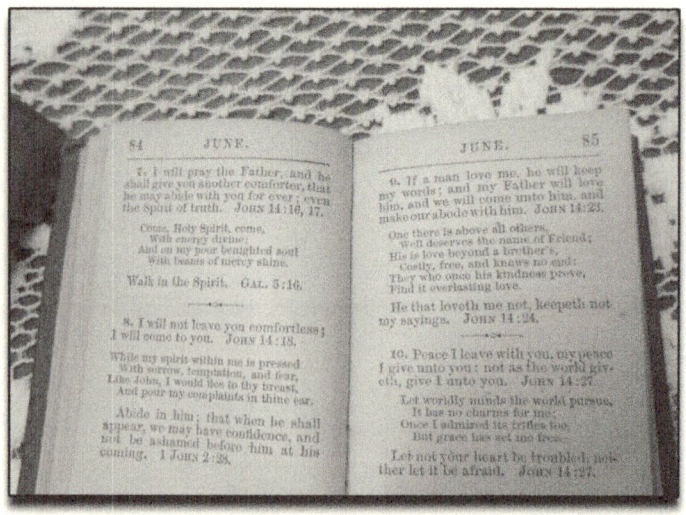

Sample pages from June.

For more titles by The Legacy of Home Press, please visit us at:

https://thelegacyofhomepress.blogspot.com

Made in United States
North Haven, CT
25 October 2024

59415503R00129